MONEY FOR TEENS

BEGINNER'S WORKBOOK

(16-19)

AEMERDALE PUBLISHING

Readers Guidelines

🛹 **PICTURE THIS: YOU KNOW THAT FEELING WHEN YOUR WI-FI GOES FROMTURTLE SPEED TO HYPERSPACE IN A BLINK? 🚀 🕹 WELL, IMAGINE MAKINGMORE MONEY IN A SINGLE MINUTE THAN YOU CAN SWIPE THROUGHINSTAGRAM IN AN HOUR! 💰🕐**

THINK ABOUT IT – THAT ADRENALINE RUSH WHEN YOU SCORE BIG IN YOURFAVORITE GAME? IMAGINE YOUR BANK ACCOUNT DOING A VICTORY DANCEBECAUSE YOU BANKED MORE MOOLAH THAN A CELEB'S SNEAKER COLLECTION COSTS! 🎮😎

IT'S LIKE SNAGGING THE FRONT ROW AT A SURPRISE VIRTUAL CONCERT WHEREYOUR FAVE ARTIST DROPS THEIR NEW TRACK BEFORE ANYONE ELSE. EXCEPT, INTHIS SCENARIO, YOUR WALLET'S THE ONE SINGING, AND IT'S HITTING THOSEHIGH NOTES OF FINANCIAL FREEDOM! 🎤🎶

We know you know everything about money; we get it.

But we think it's time that you dive into the Ultimate Investment Workbook, designed exclusively for savvy minds. 🚀

🌟 Uncover the secrets to turn your pocket change into serious gains, all while rocking that #FinancialFreedom vibe. 💸🏃

Whether you're dreaming of the latest tech, cool travel spots, or just securing your future swag, this workbook's got your back.

Turn those virtual coins into stacks you can flex, and remember, future billionaires aren't born – they're made by taking smart steps today.

So, grab your favorite caffeinated beverage, park yourself in your comfiest hangout nook, and let's crack open this workbook of financial awesomeness.

Calling all Superhero Parents!

Are you ready to empower your teens with the ultimate financial skills? This Investment Workbook isn't just for them – it's your secret weapon to guide them toward a future of financial success.

Here's how you can make the most of this game-changing resource:

1. **Team Up**: Sit down with your teens and kick-start an open convo about money matters. Embrace those awkward "money talks" and set the stage for a stronger financial future together.
2. **Tag, You're It**: Encourage your teens to dive into the workbook excitedly, but don't hesitate to jump in too! Share your insights, answer their questions, and create a dynamic learning experience. 🏃 🏃
3. **Goals Galore**: Help your teens define their dreams, from epic college adventures to cool gadgets. This workbook's all about turning those dreams into actionable goals; you can be their cheerleader.
4. **Budget BFFs**: The workbook's budgeting sections are goldmines for learning financial discipline. Show your teens how to track their spending, set allowances, and save for that next big thing.
5. **Investing Squad**: Embrace the exciting world of investing together! Break down the workbook's investment strategies, discuss the options, and help them grasp the power of compounding. 📈
6. **Celebrate Wins**: As your teens make progress, celebrate those milestones! Whether it's their first stock purchase or reaching a savings goal, your support, and enthusiasm will fuel their confidence.
7. **Stay Curious**: Keep the financial conversations flowing beyond the workbook. Share news articles, discuss market trends, and continue growing their money smarts.

Remember, you're not just teaching them about money – you're equipping them with life-changing skills. 🌟 Let's work together to nurture a generation of financially savvy individuals. Time to #ParentingWin like never before! 🎉 #FinancialFutureFam

To my husband, the ultimate saver. Your financial wisdom inspires all around. This workbook is dedicated to you, the joy of my life.

Table of Contents

Introduction

"Money is a tool. It will take you wherever you wish, but it will not replace you as the driver."
Ayn Rand

DO YOU REMEMBER THE FIRST TIME YOU SAW MONEY? AS A LITTLE KID, YOU MAY HAVE WONDERED WHY EVERYONE WAS SO EXCITED ABOUT THOSE SHINY COINS AND COLORFUL BILLS. BUT AS YOU GREW OLDER, YOU APPRECIATED ITS VALUE AND HOW IT COULD BUY YOUR FAVORITE CANDY OR TOY. AND IT FELT GOOD!

We could say that money is like a game. It's exciting and fun to play, but knowing the rules is essential if you don't want to lose. As a child, you may have thought of money simply as something to buy toys or snacks. However, as you grow older, you realize that it's much more than that.

Money can give you the freedom to pursue your dreams, but it can also lead to financial trouble if you're not careful. Making mistakes with money is all too easy, and that's why it's so crucial to learn as much as possible about managing your finances.

You're a teenager now, and you've probably got a good grasp of money, right? You know how to save for things you want and spend your cash on the latest gadgets and fashions. But here's the thing - there's so much more to money than that. Have you ever heard of credit scores, taxes, or investments? Maybe you've heard people talk about them, but do you understand what they mean?

Maybe you're a total newbie to the finance world, like the guy from that joke that thought a "stock market" was where people went to buy groceries in bulk. When he heard someone say, "I made a killing in the stock market," he imagined them walking out of the store with a cart full of food and feeling confused about how that could make someone rich.

If you're anything like him, you know there's much to learn about personal finance. Well, it's time to clear things up and discover the secrets to amazing personal finance. Whether you're a financial newbie or have some knowledge under your belt, this book will take your money understanding to the next level.

This isn't just a boring old book filled with dry financial advice. Instead, you'll find interactive quizzes and games that make learning about money fun and engaging. Plus, you'll get to read stories from real people who have successfully managed their finances and achieved their goals. You'll discover tips and tricks for earning money and smart shopping and learn about essential money-related concepts. Also, you'll get resources like cool Apps and Websites that can make managing your money easier.

In Part 1, we'll start with Money Basics. You'll learn the history and basics of money and how to budget effectively. We'll also cover the essentials of saving and investing, so you can grow your money and make it work for you.

In Part 2, we'll explore Smart Spending. We'll dive into earning money and shopping smart. You'll also learn all about credit and debt so that you can avoid those common pitfalls.

And finally, in Part 3, we'll tackle Planning for the Future. You'll discover the benefits of giving back and how to plan for college and your future career. And we won't forget about the importance of retirement planning.

As you can see, this book is your ticket to understanding personal finance from A to Z. Knowledge gives you the power to make smart decisions that lead you to your dreams. Imagine the freedom and possibilities that come with good money skills! This book will show you how to get the most out of your money and use it to propel you toward the life you deserve.

By the end of it, you'll have all the tools you need to become a money master. Remember, money is a tool that will take you wherever you wish, but it will not replace you as the driver. So, buckle up and get ready to take control of your financial future!

Reach out to
aemerdale@gmail.com
for your free answer sheet!

Chapter 1

Understanding Money

"Today, the greatest single source of
wealth is between your ears."
Brian Tracy

YOU HEAR ABOUT MONEY ALL THE TIME AND PROBABLY EVEN USE IT TO BUY LUNCH AT SCHOOL OR THINGS YOU LIKE, BUT DO YOU REALLY KNOW WHAT IT IS?

Yes, we can buy stuff with it, but there's more to it than that. Money has been around for a really long time, and it's changed a lot over the years. Today, it's not just about paper bills and shiny coins. There are digital forms of payment, like using your phone to pay for something.

Also, just like when you plant seeds in the ground and wait for them to grow into plants, you can "plant" your money in savings or investments and watch it grow over time. Like different seeds need different amounts of sunlight, water, and nutrients to grow, different financial goals and strategies require different amounts of time, effort, and resources. It's like being a gardener - you must provide the proper care and attention for your financial goals to flourish.

As you can see, money is more than what it seems. And the more you understand it, the better you get at managing it! Money is an essential part of our lives, and knowing how to handle it effectively is crucial.

In this chapter, we'll take a closer look at the definition of money and its brief history. You'll learn why money is so important and the different forms it can take. Did you know that today money comes in more than just cash? There are also credit cards, loans, and even online payments that you can use to buy things!

Most importantly, we'll talk about money management. This is a crucial part of understanding money because it's how we make sure we use our money effectively. You'll learn about the importance of managing your money and the benefits of doing it well. We'll also discuss the consequences of poor money management and how to avoid them.

So, are you curious about money and want to learn more? Get ready for an adventure into the world of finance! By the end, you'll understand what money really is and why it's vital in our lives. So, get ready to become a money master!

WHAT IS MONEY?

We use money daily, but have you ever thought about what it really is? Simply put, money is anything people use to exchange goods and services. It's a way of giving and receiving value.

But here's something interesting: even though money can be physical, like a coin or a banknote (cash), it's just a symbol of value. It represents the idea that you can exchange it for something else of value. So money is a tool we use to exchange goods and services.

Although money has changed over time, its characteristics remain the same:
- » First, it must be a medium of exchange, which means it's used for buying and selling goods or services.
- » It must be a unit of account, which means it's used to measure the value of things or to compare the prices of different goods or services.
- » It must be a store of value, saving wealth and holding purchasing power for future transactions.

To be considered money, an object or token must have all three characteristics - a medium of exchange, a unit of account, and a store of value.

To understand it better, let's say you have a collection of Pokemon cards you and your friends like to trade. These cards can be used as a medium of exchange because you can trade them for other things, like snacks or toys.

Now let's say that you and your friends agree to use a specific rare Pokemon card as a unit of account. This means that you use this card as a way to measure the value of other things you want to trade for. For example, if you want to trade for a new toy, you might say that the toy is worth two of the rare Pokemon cards.

Finally, let's say you want to save some of your Pokemon cards for later to trade with a new friend who moves to your school next year. You can use your Pokemon cards as a store of value because they can be saved and used later on to buy other things. So, your Pokemon cards can be considered "money" because they have all three characteristics: they can be used as a medium of exchange, a unit of account, and a store of value.

From Mythical Chains to Digital Coins: The Fascinating History of Money

What is the origin of the word "money"?[1] It derives from the Latin word "*moneta*," which comes from the temple of Hera the Moneta, where the Romans used to make their money in the early days of Rome.

But there's more to the origins of money! Did you know that there's a cool Greek story about how Hera, the goddess of marriage and childbirth, is connected to the origin of money? According to the story, Zeus punished Hera by tying her with a golden chain between the earth and the sky. She was alone up there, and because of this, she was called "*mone*," which means lonely. According to legend, all the gold on earth came from pieces of this golden chain that fell from the sky and became our money.

The Greeks were one of the first civilizations to use money, but they didn't use it like we do today. Gold was used only in temples, graves, and jewels. So, that's how money came to be! Pretty cool. There are also other stories about who the inventors of money were, like Demodike, Hermodike of Kyme, Lykos, Erichthonius, the Lydians, and the Naxians.

Over time, people realized that carrying heavy objects was complicated and impractical. So, they started using smaller, more convenient things like shells and beads to represent the value of goods and services. Eventually, this led to the invention of coins made out of gold, silver, and other precious metals.[2]

A Greek king named Philip II of Macedon started making golden coins around 390 BC. Before that, Greek coins were made of robust materials used to make weapons, like copper and iron. But, King Pheidon of Argos changed the coins from iron to a rather useless and ornamental metal called silver. He even dedicated some of the remaining iron coins to the temple of Hera.

Coins made trade more accessible and convenient, but people still had to carry them around, which could be dangerous. So, banks were created as a safe place to store money.

Then, in the 1600s, paper money was invented in China, which made it even easier to carry cash around. In the following graphic[2], you can see an expanded version of money's history.

Today, we use a variety of forms of money, including cash, credit cards, and digital payment systems. We can even use our phones to pay for things! Money has come a long way since the Greeks started using metal objects to trade for goods and services. It's incredible to think about how something so simple has become such an essential part of our daily lives.

So why is money so important? Without it, we wouldn't be able to buy the things we need or want. Money helps us trade goods and services without bartering or trading one thing for another. It also allows us to save for the future, invest in things we believe in, and support the causes we care about.

In conclusion, money is an integral part of our lives, and it's essential to understand what it is and how it works. From seashells to cryptocurrencies, money has taken many forms throughout history and will continue to evolve in the future.

History of Money

9000 B.C.
The earliest recorded methods of conducting transactions were gift economies and barter.

1933 A.D. - 1971
President Franklin D. Roosevelt implemented measures such as bank closures, recalling gold, and building up U.S. reserves. Later, President Richard Nixon eliminated the fixed exchange rate between gold and U.S. dollars.

1792 A.D.
The United States formalized its currency system and designated the U.S. dollar as the official currency during the coinage act of 1792.

1946 A.D.
John Biggins of the Flatbush National Bank of Brooklyn, New York, created the first bank-issued card with the "Charge-it" system.

1950 A.D.
Frank Macnamara introduced the Diners Club card, allowing cardholders to pay at restaurants and receive a bill afterward.

1100 B.C.

In China, miniature replicas of the exchanged items were used as currency, although it was inconvenient as your own money could harm you.

700 B.C.

King Alyattes of Lydia (modern-day Western Turkey) minted the first official currency, known as the Lydian Lion, which was made of a combination of silver and gold called Electrum alloy.

1200 A.D.

The introduction of paper money into Europe was influenced by Marco Polo's travels in the Asian region. However, it wasn't until 1661 that Sweden issued the first banknote.

700 A.D.

Paper money started appearing in various forms during the Song dynasty in China, but it became officially recognized during the Tang dynasty around 1100 A.D.

1990 A.D.

The merger of Confinity.com and X.com gave rise to PayPal, enabling peer-to-peer money transfers through the internet and sparking the revolution of e-wallets.

2009 A.D.

An enigmatic developer named Satoshi Nakamoto created Bitcoin, a decentralized and anonymous virtual currency.

FORMS OF MONEY

DID YOU KNOW THAT MONEY COMES IN DIFFERENT FORMS? YES, THAT'S RIGHT! MONEY CAN TAKE DIFFERENT SHAPES AND FORMS, EACH WITH UNIQUE FEATURES AND FUNCTIONS.

First off, we have cash. You're probably familiar with this one! Cash refers to physical forms of money such as coins and banknotes. Coins come in all shapes and sizes, from the tiny dime to the big, heavy dollar coin. On the other hand, banknotes are paper or plastic money issued by a central bank. You can use cash to buy things in stores, at markets, or from other people.

Next up, we have credit. Have you ever heard of a credit card? That's one type of credit. When you use a credit card, you borrow money from the bank to pay for something. You'll have to pay the bank back later, usually with some extra money added on top. Loans are another type of credit. If you need a lot of money to buy something big like a car or a house, you might take out a loan from the bank. You'll pay the loan back over time, with interest.

Now, let's hit pause for a second and talk about credit scores (an essential part of credit!). Since credit is money that financial institutions loan you in advance, they need to know your trustworthiness. Simply put, a credit score is like a report card for how responsible you are with money. It's a number that shows how likely you are to repay the borrowed money. The higher your score, the more likely banks, and other lenders will give you a loan or a credit card.

Finally, we have online transactions. These are ways to move money without using physical cash or checks. E-transfers are like sending money through the internet - you can send money to anyone with an email address. Mobile payments are another type of online transaction. You can use your phone to pay for things in stores or online. Online banking is when you use the internet to manage your money. You can check your account balance, pay bills, and transfer money between accounts.

So there you have it - the different forms of money that exist today! Whether you're using cash, credit, or online transactions, it's essential to be responsible and understand how money works.

HOW MONEY WORKS

Have you ever heard the terms "earning, spending, saving, and investing" and wondered what they really mean? These words are often thrown around regarding money, but understanding their differences is crucial in managing your finances. Our journey into the world of money begins by understanding the basics of money, including the time value of money, financial institutions like banks, and earning, spending, saving, and investing.

Money is essential to our lives, and understanding how it works can significantly benefit you. Whether you earn money through an allowance or a part-time job, knowing how to manage your finances is a valuable skill. Money is more complex than you might think! There are many things you can do with it. It's affected by time and involves different institutions.

Let's dive in and explore the various aspects of money, from earning to investing and everything in between.

IT'S ALL ABOUT EARNING, SPENDING, SAVING, AND INVESTING

Earning money is the first step toward financial independence. Whether you're doing chores around the house or working part-time, it's essential to understand the value of your time and effort. You're trading your time and skills for a reward when you earn money. The reward could be in the form of cash, a gift, or a service. Next, you'll need to decide how to use it as you earn more money.

Spending money is the most visible aspect of managing your finances. When you spend money, you use it to purchase products or services. For example, you can use your money to buy a new phone (product) or to repair your old one (service). Therefore, it's essential to be mindful of how much you're spending and what you're spending it on.

Saving money is an integral part of managing your finances. When you save money, you're setting it aside for future use. You might be saving up for a particular purchase, or you might be building an emergency fund. The key is to save consistently over time. Even small amounts can add up quickly.

Finally, investing is a way to grow your money over time. When you invest, you're using your money to purchase assets you believe will increase in value. Common investment vehicles include stocks, bonds, and mutual funds. The key to successful investing is to start early and invest consistently over time. While risks are associated with investing, the potential rewards can be significant.

We will explore each of these actions in detail in the following chapters. Upon completing this book, you will be able to manage your income like a pro!

TIME IS MONEY

Have you ever heard the phrase "time is money?" It implies that time and money go hand in hand. In fact, time and money are so closely related that understanding this relationship is essential for managing your finances effectively.

Have you ever considered why your parents encourage you to save your allowance money instead of spending it all at once? It's because of something called the time value of money. This concept means that the value of money changes over time. In other words, the money you have today is worth more than the same amount of money you will have in the future.

Let's say you have $10 and can invest it to earn interest. After a year, your $10 will have grown to $11. The $1 you made is the interest or the price of waiting one year to get your money back. This is because, during that year, you could have used that money to buy things, but instead, you chose to invest it to earn more money in the future.

Financial experts use a time value of money calculator tool to determine how much money will be worth in the future. The calculator considers factors such as the interest rate and the time that has passed since the investment was made.

Understanding the time value of money is crucial because it can help you make better financial decisions. For example, it can help you decide whether to save or spend your money, and it can also help you determine whether an investment is worth it.

FROM WHERE DOES THE MONEY COME, AND WHERE DOES IT GO? FINANCIAL INSTITUTIONS 101

We work hard to earn money, spend it on things we need or want, save it for rainy days, and invest it to make it grow. From buying your favorite gadget to saving up for a car, money is at the center of it all. But have you ever thought about the role of institutions involved in managing your money? Financial institutions are an essential part of the financial system, from banks to credit unions.

Financial institutions play a crucial role in the economy. The most known are banks. These institutions provide a range of services to individuals and businesses. Their services include checking and savings accounts, loans, and credit cards. Banks make money by charging interest on loans and investing the funds their customers deposited. Using a bank lets you keep your money safe and earn interest on your savings.

But there, our financial system goes beyond banks. There are several types of financial institutions, each with unique features and functions. Here are some others besides banks.

» Credit unions: These are similar to banks but are member-owned and typically offer lower fees and interest rates than banks.

» Investment banks: These institutions specialize in helping companies raise capital by underwriting and selling securities such as stocks and bonds.

» Brokerage firms: These firms facilitate the buying and selling of stocks, bonds, and other securities on behalf of clients.

» Insurance companies: These institutions provide various types of insurance, such as life, health, auto, and home insurance.

» Mutual funds: These investment companies pool money from many investors and invest it in a diversified portfolio of stocks, bonds, and other securities.

» Hedge funds: These are investment partnerships that are generally only available to wealthy individuals and institutions, and they invest in various assets to generate high returns.

» Venture capital firms: These institutions provide funding to startup companies that they believe have high growth potential in exchange for an ownership stake in the company.

Understanding the different financial institutions might not seem important to you right now, but trust me, the knowledge will come in handy sooner or later. When it comes to money, managing it well is key, and that starts with understanding how it works. It's important to know where to go when you need a loan, where to deposit your money to earn interest, or where to invest your savings to make it grow. You want to avoid being caught off-guard when unexpected expenses arise or when you want to take advantage of investment opportunities.

In conclusion, managing your finances is an essential part of growing up. By earning money, spending wisely, saving consistently, and investing over time, you can build a solid financial foundation for your future. Understanding the time value of money and the role of financial institutions can help you make better financial decisions. Remember, every financial decision you make has an impact on your future, so choose wisely.

MANAGING YOUR MONEY

Money management is an essential life skill that will benefit you in the long run. As a teenager, it may not seem like you have much money to manage, but starting to develop good money habits now will help you throughout your life. When you manage your money effectively, you will be able to achieve your financial goals and have financial security.

There are several benefits to good money management. You will be able to budget your money effectively, meaning you know how much money you have coming in and going out. This will help you prioritize your spending and avoid overspending. Money management also involves saving money regularly, which will help you reach your financial goals, like buying a car, traveling, or saving for college. When you have a solid financial foundation, you will be able to enjoy life's pleasures without worrying about your finances.

On the other hand, poor money management can lead to many negative consequences. Overspending, not budgeting, or not saving can lead to financial stress, debt, and even bankruptcy. Living paycheck to paycheck can make you feel trapped and unable to enjoy life's little joys. When you don't have control over your finances, it can affect other areas of your life, such as your relationships, health, and overall well-being.

In conclusion, managing your money effectively is essential to achieving financial security and goals. Good money management involves budgeting, saving, and investing your money wisely. By managing your money effectively, you can enjoy life's pleasures without worrying about your finances.

Fill in the Blanks Fun

FILL IN THE MISSING WORDS IN EACH GIVEN SENTENCE.

» _____ is anything that people use to exchange goods and services.

» Money has three characteristics: It must be a medium of exchange, a _____, and a store of value.

» Your _____ is a number that shows how likely you are to pay back the money you've borrowed.

» _____ is a Latin word that means the place where the Romans used to make their money.

» A Greek king named Philip II of Macedon started making _____ around 390 BC.

» _____ was used for coins before silver.

» _____ are similar to banks, but they are member-owned and typically offer lower fees and interest rates than banks.

» The _____ is the concept that the value of money changes over time.

» _____ is a way to grow your money over time by purchasing assets that you believe will increase in value.

CHAPTER 1

Key takeaways

» Money is anything people use to exchange goods and services. It's a way of giving and receiving value.

» Even though money can be physical, like a coin or a banknote (cash), it's just a symbol of value. It must be a medium of exchange, a unit of account and a store of value

» Money derives from the Latin word "*moneta*" and comes in different forms. You have cash (physical forms of money such as coins and banknotes), credit (Such as a credit card or loans) and online transaction (sending money through the internet)

» Earning, spending, saving and investing are the ways to use your money.

» Earning money is the first step toward financial independence. With a good job you can earn some money.

» Spending money is all about getting to use that money by buying something . Saving money is managing your money correctly so you can have some money separated to use for a goal you have, or an emergency. Investing is a way to grow your money over time.

» Time and money are so closely related that understanding this relationship is essential for managing your finances effectively. The value of money changes over time. In other words, the money you have today is worth more than the same amount of money you will have in the future.

» Financial institutions play a crucial role in the economy. There are credit unions which offer lower fees and interest rates than banks. Investment banks that specialize in helping companies raise capital by underwriting and selling securities such as stocks and bonds. Brokerage firm that facilitate the buying and selling of stocks, bonds, and other securities on behalf of clients and others such as, insurance companies, mutual funds, hedge funds, venture capital firms.

1 Academickids. (n.d.). Money. In Academic Kids Encyclopedia. Retrieved March 6, 2023, from https://academickids.com/encyclopedia/index.php/Money
2 Trading Bible. (2021). History of Money [Image]. Retrieved from https://thetradingbible.com/history-of-money.

Chapter 2

Budgeting

" A budget is telling your money where to go
instead of wondering where it went."
John C. Maxwell

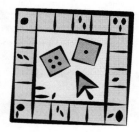

IF YOU'VE EVER PLAYED MONOPOLY, YOU KNOW THAT IT'S NOT JUST A GAME OF LUCK. INSTEAD, IT'S A GAME OF STRATEGY.

In this cool and classic board game, you have a set amount of money and must make strategic decisions about spending and saving it. It seems simple at first, but when the dices start rolling, obstacles appear, such as landing on properties with high rent or drawing a card that requires payment. This is where prioritizing your spending becomes crucial, just like in real life.

In Monopoly, it will all come down to your strategy. You can grow your wealth and win by prioritizing your spending, saving, and investing wisely. The problem is that you may end up bankrupt if you don't make smart choices along the way.

In real life, budgeting works similarly. Setting financial goals and making smart spending decisions can help you manage your money. Just like Monopoly, budgeting requires prioritization - figuring out what expenses are necessary and what can be cut. It also involves investing in the right things, like education or a savings account, to grow your wealth. Having a budget isn't just about saving money but also about feeling secure and having peace of mind.

Like Monopoly, budgeting can be tough, but it's well worth it. In the following pages, we'll go over everything you need to know about budgeting, like how to create one, track expenses, and make smart financial decisions. Suppose you're new to budgeting or looking to improve your financial management skills. In that case, this chapter will provide you with the tools and insights you need to succeed. Get ready to roll your dice - it's time to start budgeting!

BUDGETING 101

A study[1] by the University of Arizona a few years ago found that teenagers who got financial education and budgeted were more likely to save money, take on less debt, and have better credit scores than their peers who didn't. The effort is worth it!

Many studies over the years and around the world have found that budgeting in your teen years affects your financial well-being later in life. Developing good financial habits at a young age can set you up for a lifetime of success.

WHAT'S A BUDGET?

Getting your first paycheck is so exciting! You can do so many things with that money; new clothes, saving for a car, eating out. But if you don't watch yourself, it will be spent as soon as it gets into your pocket. That's why we have budgets! Setting a budget and sticking to it can make you enjoy your money to the best of your ability while also keeping room to save some of it for the future.

In reality, a budget is just a plan for how you will spend your money. In a personal budget, you estimate your income and expenses for a particular period (usually a month). The goal is to understand how you spend your money and manage it better, so you can save and achieve short-, medium-, and long-term goals, such as buying a car or going on a trip. A budget will also help you reduce stress in your day to day, at least when it comes to money.

A budget is just a plan for how you will spend your money.

We can summarize the main advantages of budgeting in three points.

MOTIVATION	**VISIBILITY**	**SECURITY**
Saving for a specific goal is a great motivator to keep you from overspending in the short term.	If you know exactly how much you're spending in different areas, you can make any changes, like cutting back on eating out.	Budgeting for essentials and avoiding discretionary purchases gives you a safety net you can use anytime.

But that's not it. You'll see many changes in your everyday life by budgeting during your teen years, including

» You'll understand where your money comes from.
Budgeting can help you understand your income sources, such as allowances, part-time jobs, or family gifts. You'll appreciate your earnings more if you understand where your money comes from.

» You'll be able to track expenses and stay on budget.
Budgeting helps you keep track of your expenses and stay within your budget. Doing this can prevent overspending and avoid unexpected expenses or financial emergencies. You can determine if you are overspending by tracking your expenses and adjusting your budget accordingly.

» You'll learn to set long-term financial goals.
By learning to budget, you can set long-term financial goals, such as saving for college or a car. Setting objectives makes you focus more on meeting that horizon and thus follow the previous budget more enthusiastically. Reaching the goal (no matter how small) will give you a sense of reaching a milestone and encourage you to set bigger goals in the future.

» You'll distinguish between good and bad debts.

By budgeting, you can distinguish between good debts, such as student loans or mortgages, and bad debts, such as credit card debt. You can avoid high-interest debt pitfalls if you know how to distinguish between the two.

» You'll learn to buy only when your need is real.

It is common today to buy things simply because we want them rather than because they are necessities. There's a fine line between "need" and "desire"; knowing the difference is key. By setting a budget, you can develop a healthier attitude towards spending by only buying things you need. Maintaining a healthy financial lifestyle is easier if you avoid impulse purchases and focus on actual needs.

» You'll understand the importance of saving and having an emergency fund.

Lastly, budgeting can help you appreciate the benefits of saving money, such as having funds available for emergencies or achieving long-term financial goals. Putting aside funds for unexpected expenses, like car repairs or medical bills, can help reduce stress and financial strain. An emergency fund can give you peace of mind and help you prepare for anything.

Are you ready to take control of your financial future? All it takes is honesty with yourself and determination. Taking a look at your bills, everyday expenses, and future goals is an excellent place to start. Luckily, with the convenience of online banking and mobile apps, you can easily get a clear view of your money situation. Don't worry, we'll cover these tools later. But for now, let's dive into some simple steps to create your personal budget.

CREATING A PERSONAL BUDGET

We all need to see where our money goes every month. We've seen that a budget helps you feel more in control of your finances and may even let you save money. Keeping track of your finances is key. Here's how to make a budget in five simple steps.

STEP 1: CALCULATE YOUR INCOME

Your net income is the foundation of your budget. Simply put, income refers to the money that you receive regularly. Net income is what you take home after tax and employer-provided benefits like retirement plans and health insurance. Focusing on your total salary instead of net income could lead you to overspend because you think you have more money than you really do. For now, you probably don't have to worry about this. You should just know that deductions exist.

Making a budget that accounts for how much money you have coming in each month can be easy when you know your sources of income.

Sources of income

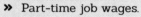

In your teen years, you can earn money in a variety of ways:

- » Part-time job wages.
- » Allowances from parents or other family members.
- » Money earned from babysitting or pet-sitting.
- » Income from a small business (e.g., selling handmade crafts online).
- » Cash gifts for special occasions (e.g., birthdays, holidays).
- » Scholarships or bursaries for academic or sports achievements.
- » Prize money from contests or competitions.
- » Tips earned from working in the service industry (e.g., restaurants, hair salons).

By tracking your income and expenses, you can ensure you're not overspending and save money for the things that matter most to you. Therefore, it is essential to keep detailed records of your different income streams to manage your variable earnings efficiently.

STEP 2: TRACK YOUR SPENDING

Once you know how much money you're getting, the next step is to figure out where it's going. Tracking and categorizing your spending can help you determine where you're spending the most and where you can save. There are two main types of expenses in finance: fixed expenses and variable expenses.

Fixed expenses

» Remain the same every month.
» These are generally contractual or committed expenses that are difficult to change in the short term.
» Often include payments for rent/mortgage, car payments, insurance premiums, and subscriptions.
» They are usually necessary for daily living and stability.
» Require planning and budgeting to ensure they are paid on time.

Variable expenses

» It can change from month to month.
» Include discretionary spending on things like groceries, entertainment, and transportation.
» Often depends on individual lifestyle choices and preferences.
» It can be adjusted based on needs and priorities.
» It may require more monitoring and control to avoid overspending.

Fixed expenses

Variable expenses

Make a list of your fixed expenses first. These are regular monthly spendings like phone bills, car payments, or subscriptions for streaming services, magazines, or music services. Next, prepare a list of your variable expenses, which can vary from month to month, such as clothing purchases, eating out, and entertainment. You may be able to reduce expenses in this area. If you have a credit card statement, that's an excellent place to start, as they often break down your monthly expenses by category.

HOW TO KEEP TRACK OF YOUR DAILY EXPENSES?

Keeping track of your daily expenses has always been challenging. But, Modern technology provides you with many apps for your mobile phone that let you track your expenses and income daily.

You'll see how useful these tools are throughout the month so you don't get overwhelmed. Of course, you can also use your usual pen and paper, even a calculation document you fill out daily or every few days. However, I encourage you to try the apps at the end of this chapter since they will help you keep track of your expenses in real-time.

STEP 3: SET REALISTIC GOALS

Make a list of your financial goals before reviewing the data you've tracked. By setting goals, you can create a roadmap for your finances and work towards achieving the essential things for you. There are two types of financial goals: short-term and long-term. You want to achieve short-term goals soon, typically within a year or less. However, you want to accomplish long-term goals over a more extended period, such as five or ten years.

» Short-term financial goals could be saving for a new phone, a trip with friends, or buying a concert ticket. These goals are achievable within a relatively short period and can provide a sense of accomplishment and motivation.

» Long-term financial goals include saving for college tuition or a down payment on a future home. These goals require more planning and commitment but can significantly impact your future financial stability.

Remember, your goals don't have to be final, but identifying them can motivate you to stay within your budget. For example, it may be easier to cut back if you know you're saving for a scooter or summer vacation with your friends.

STEP 4: BRING IT ALL TOGETHER

This is the point where your actual spending meets your desired spending. Now is the time to analyze your current financial situation.

As you know your fixed and variable expenses, you can get an idea of what you'll spend in the coming months. Also, being familiar with your sources of income and goals will help you organize your priorities.

For example, let's say you have a part-time job that pays you $200 monthly. You have fixed expenses such as your phone bill, which is $50 a month, and your transportation expenses, which are around $40 a month. Additionally, you have variable expenses, such as eating out and going to the movies, which can vary from $50 to $100 a month. By creating a budget, you can see that you'll have around $60 to $110 left for savings, depending on how much you spend on variable expenses.

You get a clearer picture of your financial health at this point. It's essential to take a step back and analyze your spending habits so that you can make changes where necessary. If you find that you're spending more than what is coming in, don't worry! This is a common issue that can be fixed with some budgeting strategies.

STEP 5: ADJUST YOUR SPENDING TO STAY ON BUDGET

Once you've documented your income and expenses, you can make adjustments to ensure you spend wisely and have money for your goals. There may be some variable expenses you can cut back on. For example, can you skip going to the movies one night and watch a movie at home?

Consider adjusting your fixed expenses if the numbers still don't add up. Could you, for example, save more by looking for a better price on your phone plan? These decisions come with significant trade-offs, so carefully weigh your options. Remember, even small savings can add up to a lot of money. You'll be surprised how much more money you can save with a few minor adjustments.

The 50/30/20 rule

You may be struggling with reorganizing your expenses after reviewing your finances. Luckily, there are many tools and answers to help us succeed in the world of money. The 50/30/20 rule might make your life easier.

You can think of the 50/30/30 rule as a budgeting guideline that suggests dividing your income into three groups:

1. Necessities: This category should make up 50% of your income and includes essential expenses like rent, utilities, groceries, transportation costs, and any other bills you absolutely need to pay.

2. Discretionary spending: Expenses in this category should make up 30% of your income. In this section, you'll consider all the fun stuff, like eating out, entertainment, hobbies, and travel. Keep track of your spending in this category to stay within budget!

3. Savings and debt repayment: The rule affirms that 20% of your income should be devoted to this category. It includes putting money aside for emergencies, retirement, or any other long-term goals you might have. In addition, use this category to pay off any outstanding debt, like credit card balances or student loans, so you don't get weighed down by interest.

The 50/30/20 method can be a great way to organize your spending. The plan is simple to follow and easy to customize for your spending habits and goals. You can make the most of this flexible set of guidelines by adapting it to your needs.

Saving 20% might be unrealistic for you, but with this budget, you can use the figures as a guide and tweak them to make sense for you. This rule involves setting yourself a monthly savings goal and actively adjusting your spending to meet it.

REVIEW YOUR BUDGET REGULARLY

Once you have a budget, it's essential to constantly monitor your spending to ensure you're on track. Budgets aren't final. You could get an extra income, your expenses might change, or you may reach your goal and want to set another one. Whatever the reason, review your budget periodically by following the steps above.

THE BEST BUDGETING APPS

It can be a daunting task to keep track of all your income and expenses manually. Fortunately, several budgeting apps are available to make the process much easier and more efficient. Below are a few of the most recommended budgeting apps:

» PocketGuard: With PocketGuard, you can easily track your expenses and create personalized budgets. Plus, it offers suggestions for saving money and provides insights into your spending patterns.

» Mint: Mint is a popular finance app that sends alerts to help you stay on track with your budgeting goals. You can easily track your expenses, monitor your credit score, and create budgets.

» YNAB (You Need a Budget): YNAB helps you create and stick to a budget while offering financial education and guidance. It's perfect for teenagers who want to make informed financial decisions.

» Goodbudget: Goodbudget uses the envelope budgeting method to help you manage your money. You can allocate funds to different categories and track your spending accordingly.

» Wally: Wally is a free app that tracks your expenses and creates budgets. It also offers features such as receipt scanning and savings goal tracking.

Get to work!

CREATE A PERSONALIZED PLAN TO ANALYZE YOUR FINANCES AND DECIDE WHERE TO PUT YOUR MONEY.

Here's a template to help you start building a solid foundation for your finances.

MONTHLY BUDGET PLANNER

Month _____

Initial Balance _____

Monthly Goals _____

Income

Date	Source	Amount
	Total:	

Notes

Fixed Expenses

Date	Source	Amount
	Total:	

Variable Expenses

Date	Source	Amount
	Total:	

Debts

Date	Source	Amount
	Total:	

Summary

Source	Amount
(+) Income	
(-) Fixed Expenses	
(-) Variable Expenses	
(-) Debts	
Total:	

In conclusion, sticking to a budget can be challenging, but the benefits are well worth the effort. By setting a budget and tracking your expenses, you can gain control over your finances and make more informed financial decisions. However, it is important to be aware of the challenges that come with budgeting, such as unexpected expenses and the temptation to overspend.

In the long run, sticking to a budget can reduce debt and increase savings, making you feel better financially.

CHAPTER 2

Key takeaways

» A budget is just a plan for how you will spend your money. In a personal budget, you estimate your income and expenses for a particular period. It can help you reduce stress in your day to day, at least when it comes to money.

» The goal is to understand how you spend your money and manage it better, so you can save and achieve short-, medium-, and long-term goals, such as buying a car or going on a trip.

» Some advantages are motivation, visibility and security. You will also, understand where your money comes from, track expenses and learn to set long-term financial goals

» To create your personal budget, you should calculate your income, check your sources of income, track your spending, set realistic goals, and adjust your spending to stay on budget.

» The 50/30/20 rule as a budgeting guideline suggests dividing your income into three groups. The first group is necessities, that should make up 50% and are expenses like rent, utilities, groceries. The second group is discretionary spending, 30% of your income, which stands for fun stuff, like eating out, entertainment, hobbies, and travel. And the last one is savings and debt repayment which is 20% of your income.

» The best budgeting apps are: PocketGuard, Mint, YNAB, Goodbudget, Wally.

---

1 Hira, T.K., Mugenda, O.M., & Mugo, M. (2000). Financial management practices and financial well-being of Kenyan urban households. Journal of Consumer Affairs, 34(1), 1-20. https://doi.org/10.1111/j.1745-6606.2000.tb00001.x

Chapter 3

Saving and Investing

"Risk comes from not
knowing what you're doing."
Warren Buffett

YOU'VE PROBABLY SEEN THE DISNEY MOVIE UP. BUT IF YOU HAVEN'T, YOU SHOULD! IT IS A HEARTWARMING STORY THAT TEACHES YOU THAT YOU CAN MOVE YOUR HOUSE ANYWHERE WITH ENOUGH BALLOONS AND AN ESSENTIAL LESSON ABOUT PERSONAL FINANCES.

Carl and Ellie wanted to travel to Paradise Falls. Still, their lack of an emergency fund prevented them from doing so. Every time something happened, their money was gone, and they had to start over. Up shows us that a good understanding of saving is the best way to make our dreams come true.

Suppose you're working hard to make money. In that case, the day will probably come when you have more money than you need to cover your fixed and variable expenses (congrats! Now you know what those are). As a result, you'll have extra money to use. It is at this point that saving and investing become essential concepts. The smartest thing you can do when you're young is to save and invest.

You're probably thinking – "Investing and saving? That sounds boring and complicated." But trust me, it's not as difficult as it seems. Investing simply means putting your money to work for you by buying assets that can earn you more money over time. And saving means setting aside a portion of your income for future use.

So, why should you care about investing and saving as a teenager? Well, the earlier you start, the more time your money has to grow. Investing and saving wisely as a teenager can prevent you from falling into what Carl and Ellie had to experience, which is not being able to make their dreams come true. So, in this chapter, we'll show you how to save and invest like a boss and achieve your goals.

SAVINGS AND INVESTING: WHAT'S THE DEAL?

To be a rockstar at managing your finances, you must understand the value of saving and investing. These two things can be a game-changer for your financial future and set you up for success in the long run.

So, why do people save and invest? Most people do this to achieve a specific goal, such as buying a car, going to college, or starting a family. But there's more to saving and investing than just short-term goals. It's also about planning for the future! One of the most important reasons to save and invest is to ensure you have enough money for a comfortable retirement when you're older. It may seem far away now, but your future self will thank you. In addition, if you save and invest for the long term, you'll make more money through things like interest and stock market returns. You might think that sounds complicated but don't worry. We'll guide you every step of the way.

Saving

» You save money when you set aside money you won't spend now for emergencies or future purchases.
» Financial institutions offer several different savings options.
» Your "savings" are usually put in safe places or products that can be accessed anytime. Among the savings products are savings accounts, checking accounts, and certificates of deposit.

Investing

» In investing, you purchase assets such as stocks, bonds, mutual funds, or real estate with the expectation they will make money for you.
» Investments usually are selected to achieve long-term goals.
» Generally speaking, investments can be categorized as income Investments or growth investments.

There is a greater risk of losing your money when you invest than when you save, but you also have the opportunity to earn more money.

Let's say you want to buy a new phone that costs $500. You have $100 in your pocket, but you must save the rest before purchasing the phone. So, you start saving money by putting $20 in a jar weekly. After 20 weeks of saving, you've reached your goal and have $500 to buy the phone!

You want to save for something bigger, like a car. A car can cost thousands of dollars, so it would take a lot longer to save up enough money just by putting your money in a jar. That's where investing comes in. Investing is when you place your money into something that has the potential to grow in value over time, like stocks or mutual funds.

So, instead of saving your money in a jar, you could invest some of it in a mutual fund. You'll learn more about mutual funds later. In the meantime, just know that a mutual fund's value could increase over time, making your investment worth more than you put into it. You could save up for a car much faster with that extra money!

So, that's the difference between saving and investing. Saving is when you put money aside for a specific goal, like buying a phone. Investing is when you put money into something that has the potential to grow in value over time, like a mutual fund, to help you reach bigger financial goals in the future.

WHY SHOULD I CARE ABOUT SAVING AND INVESTING?

In the same way that physical activity and vegetables are good for your health, saving and investing play a crucial role in your financial well-being. You must learn to save periodically and invest wisely to achieve your goals.

For many reasons, saving and investing will make a big difference in your future. For instance, an emergency fund is essential for unexpected events like job loss, medical emergencies, or car repairs. You can avoid financial stress during challenging times by having a savings account with three to six months of living expenses.

And don't forget about retirement! Investing in a retirement account like a 401(k) or IRA can help ensure financial security during your golden years. The earlier you start saving, the more your money can grow through the power of compounding.

Before retiring, you may dream of owning a house or car or attending a good college. Saving for significant purchases like those is also a smart move. By doing this, you'll be able to reduce debt and rely less on loans. Plus, saving and investing can help you achieve financial independence, providing more flexibility in your career and life choices.

The benefits of saving and investing

By saving up over time, you can achieve your goals and even afford those big-ticket items like a car or a home. Plus, having an emergency fund can help you be prepared for unexpected expenses like a medical emergency or car repair. And when opportunities come up, like a chance to travel or help others, you can do it without worrying about going into debt. Having money available can give you peace of mind and make you worry less about money matters. So why not start saving today and reap the benefits for years to come?

SAVING

Because your priority is not working during adolescence, you might be unable to save much money in your teens. However, it's the best time to learn about how saving works, and you might be able to save a little money if you use the proper methods to save. To begin, let's look at how people save money.

DIFFERENT TYPES OF SAVINGS ACCOUNTS

By keeping your money in a savings account, it will stay safe, and you will also earn a little bit of extra money on top of what you already have.

In most cases, it takes place at a bank or credit union, which you already know are places that help you manage your finances.

While you won't make a ton of money from having a savings account, it's a good option to save money for something you want to buy shortly, like a new video game or a pair of shoes. And because it's a safe and reliable way to store your money, you don't have to worry about losing it.

There are different types of savings accounts.

HIGH-YIELD SAVINGS ACCOUNTS

These are like regular savings accounts but offer higher interest rates. That means you can earn more money on the money you save. Another good thing about them is that they are available through online banks. High-yield savings accounts may also have fewer fees than traditional savings accounts.

If you want to earn more interest on your savings, a high-yield savings account might be a good choice. For example, a high-yield savings account might help you reach your goal faster if you're saving up for a new video game.

MONEY MARKET ACCOUNTS

These accounts are similar to high-yield savings accounts but offer a higher interest rate, which means they are an opportunity for making more money. Nonetheless, it requires a higher minimum balance to open and maintain the performance (you must have more money to open and keep them). It may restrict the number of withdrawals or transfers allowed per month.

This is an excellent option for someone saving up for a specific goal, like a summer vacation.

CERTIFICATE OF DEPOSIT (CD) ACCOUNTS

These accounts require you to keep your money in the account for a set amount of time, like a few months or years. But in exchange for leaving your money there, the bank usually gives you a higher interest rate than a regular savings account. Just be careful, because if you take your money out, you might have to pay a fee.

If you have some money that you know you won't need for a while, a CD account might be a good way to earn a little extra interest. For example, suppose you just got a big inheritance and didn't need the money immediately. In that case, a CD account might be an excellent place to put it.

INDIVIDUAL RETIREMENT ACCOUNTS (IRAS)

These are special savings accounts just for retirement. There are two main kinds: traditional and Roth. With traditional IRAs, you put money in before you pay taxes, which can lower how much you have to pay in taxes overall. With Roth IRAs, you put in cash after you've paid taxes, but you might not have to pay taxes on the money you take out when you retire.

IRAs are best for people who want to save money for retirement. This means that an IRA can be a great option if you're young and want to start saving for when you're older.

HEALTH SAVINGS ACCOUNTS (HSAS)

You can use these savings accounts to pay for medical expenses if you have a high-deductible health insurance plan. You can put money in before you pay taxes, which can help lower how much you have to pay in taxes overall. And when you take the money out to pay for medical expenses, you don't have to pay taxes on it. This is a great way to save money for medical costs while also saving money on taxes.

Once you start saving, you may feel overwhelmed by all the options. But don't worry; you just need to find the savings account that fits you like a glove! It's like shopping for the perfect outfit; you want something that looks great and feels comfortable but also suits the occasion. The same goes for savings accounts; you want something that works for your situation. So look at your needs, and choose the version that fits you best. Your financial success begins with the correct savings account!

WHAT'S THE BEST WAY TO START SAVING MONEY AS A TEENAGER?

First, figuring out what you want to save for is essential. You may want to save up for a new video game or have your sights set on a big purchase like a car or a trip. Whatever it is, set a goal for yourself and keep reminding yourself of it to stay motivated to save.

Once you know what you want to save money for, the first step is to start separating your spending money from your savings. This means having two different bank accounts, one for spending and one for saving. Creating this separation can help you resist the temptation to dip into your savings for everyday expenses like going to the movies or eating out with friends. For example, you can put your allowance or part-time job earnings into your savings account and then transfer a set amount to your spending account each week.

By setting a goal and separating your spending money from your savings, you'll be well on your way to building a healthy savings habit that will serve you well throughout your life.

The Smart Way to Save

Let's say you've worked hard all week. You've washed cars, babysat, or done chores at home to earn extra money. It can be hard to resist spending that money all at once on something you know will make you really happy as soon as you get your hands on it. That is when the term delayed gratification comes in hand. This means putting your future before your wants is a challenge. For this reason, you have to be very smart when doing so. One way to help motivate yourself to save is to reward yourself.

When you set goals for your savings, it can feel like a never-ending journey with no end in sight. However, you can break up the trip and celebrate your progress by rewarding yourself for reaching milestones. For example, saving $100 could reward yourself with a small treat or indulgence, like a movie or a new piece of clothing.

But rewards don't have to be material things. For example, rewarding yourself with a sense of accomplishment or pride in reaching your goals can also be helpful. This can keep you motivated and remind you of your progress.

Another important aspect of saving is removing obstacles that can get in the way of your progress. Thankfully, you are not alone on this! Technology has your back. What does that mean, exactly?

Thanks to technology, you can now set up your account to automatically move money into a separate savings or investment account or pay regular bills without remembering to do it every month. This means you won't have to worry about forgetting to save or pay bills on time, and you can focus on achieving your goals.

So, how can you automate your savings? Here are a few ideas:
- » Set up a regular transfer from your checking account into a savings account. This can be done weekly or monthly, and it can be for any amount that you choose.
- » Use an app that automatically rounds up your purchases to the nearest dollar and saves the extra change. Some apps even invest the extra change for you!

By automating your savings, you'll remove the obstacles in your way and make it easier to reach your goals.

By now, you've definitely mastered the art of saving. But as I said at the beginning of the chapter, that's not the only way you can grow your money. Investing and saving can help you grow your wealth over time, but they have risks and work differently.

In contrast to saving, investing involves higher risk and greater potential returns. This is why understanding how it works is so crucial. The risk is higher, so make sure you know what you're doing.

INVESTING

There are two ways to make money: You work for money, or your money works for you. In the first case, someone pays you to work for them, or you have your own business. In the second, you take your money and save or invest it. Before diving into the exciting world of investing, you need to understand a few key things.

Firstly, it's essential to grasp the relationship between risk and return. In the world of investing, higher returns often come with higher risks. Understanding this connection can help you make informed decisions about which investments to pursue.

Next, various investment vehicles are available, from stocks and bonds to mutual funds and real estate. Each comes with risks and potential rewards, and it's crucial to understand the differences between them to choose the best option for you.

And let's not forget about diversification. This simply means spreading your investments across multiple asset classes in order to reduce risk. By diversifying your portfolio, you can help protect yourself against market fluctuations and potentially increase your overall returns.

So, as you can see, there's a lot to consider when it comes to investing. But don't worry. We'll start with the basics and guide you through each step of the way!

THE RISK-RETURN EQUATION

Investing beginners should understand that risk and opportunity go hand in hand when getting started. All investments involve taking on risks. Therefor, it's important that you go into any investment in stocks, bonds, or mutual funds with a full understanding that you could lose some or all of your money in any one investment.

When deciding to invest, it is essential to understand the relationship between risk and return. Generally, higher-risk investments can pay off more but can also lose a lot. The returns on low-risk investments tend to be lower, but they're more stable and secure.

If you're considering investing, you need to know your risk tolerance. Younger people may have a higher risk tolerance and can take on more risk in investments. To protect their savings, older people might prefer lower-risk investments.

What you need to know about risk tolerance

Simply put, "risk tolerance" is a fancy way of describing how much risk you're willing to take with your money when investing. It means figuring out how comfortable you are with the possibility of losing some of your money to gain more in the long run.

A good way of understanding it is the TikTok trend of being offered a mystery box in exchange for a dollar. Many people love surprises and don't mind taking a gamble, so they choose the mystery box even though they don't know what's inside. Sometimes they get more money or something really cool like a phone. But other times, they get nothing. Some people are not big fans of uncertainty and prefer to stick with what they know, so they choose to keep their dollar.

Now, let's talk about "risk capacity." This refers to how much financial wiggle room you have when it comes to investing. For instance, if you're already doing well financially and have some extra money to spare, you might be able to afford taking on more risk with your investments. However, if you're barely making ends meet and can't afford to lose any money, you'll likely want to play it safe and avoid high-risk investments.

Following the example above, the risk of a dollar when you only have three dollars differs from the risk of a dollar after you have three hundred dollars.

So, figuring out your risk tolerance and risk capacity is all about finding a balance between taking chances and being financially responsible. Just like with the dollar and the mystery box, when you invest, it's important to weigh the potential rewards against the possible risks and make a decision that feels right for you.

INVESTMENT VEHICLES

An investment vehicle is a product used by investors to gain positive returns. Investment vehicles can be low risks, such as certificates of deposit (CDs) or bonds, or they can carry a greater degree of risk, such as stocks, options, and futures.

STOCKS

Imagine you and your friends starting a lemonade stand together. You each put in some money to buy supplies and set up the stand, but you all own different parts of the business. That's kind of like what a stock is. When you buy a stock, you become a part-owner of a company, and if the company makes money, you can make money too! But if the company doesn't do well, the value of your stock might go down. It's like playing a game of chance, but you can learn how to play safely by using a practice account.

BONDS

A bond is like a loan you give to a company or the government. They promise to pay you back the money you lent them plus some extra money, called interest. It's like you're the bank, and they're the ones borrowing from you. It's not as exciting as stocks, but it's a great way to save money and earn a little extra cash.

TAX-FREE SAVINGS ACCOUNT (TFSA)

It's like a piggy bank but for grown-ups. You can put money into the account, invest it, and watch it grow over time. The cool thing about a TFSA is that you don't have to pay taxes on the money you earn. It's like getting a free pass from the government!

MUTUAL FUNDS

They're like a big bag of candy that lots of people share. You and a bunch of other people put your money together, and a professional money manager uses that money to buy a bunch of different stocks, bonds, and other investments. This is a great way to invest in many different companies without buying each stock individually.

EXCHANGE-TRADED FUNDS (ETFS)

They're like a basket of different goodies, like a gift basket. You buy one ETF with many different stocks, bonds, or other investments inside. They're a safer way to invest in the stock market because they're diversified, meaning you're not just relying on one company to do well.

HOW TO CHOOSE THE RIGHT INVESTMENT VEHICLE

The answer depends on when you will need the money, your goals, and if you will be able to sleep at night if you purchase a risky investment where you could lose your principal.

If you are saving for retirement, and you have 35 years before you retire, you may want to consider riskier investment products, knowing that if you stick to only the "savings" products or to less risky investment products, your money will grow too slowly—or, given inflation and taxes, you may lose the purchasing power of your money. A frequent mistake people make is putting the money they will not need for a very long time into investments that pay a low amount of interest.

On the other hand, if you are saving for a short-term goal, five years or less, you don't want to choose risky investments because when it's time to sell, you may have to take a loss. Since investments often move up and down in value rapidly, you want to make sure that you can wait and sell at the best possible time.

 ## Diversification

Diversification is a key concept in investing that can be summed up by the age-old saying, "Don't put all your eggs in one basket." This means that you should not concentrate all your resources, whether they be money, time, or energy, into a single investment or venture. Instead, it's wise to spread out your investments across different sectors and asset classes.

Diversification is important for several reasons.

» It helps to mitigate risks.

If you invest all your money into one stock and that company experiences financial difficulties, your entire investment could be wiped out. On the other hand, if you diversify your portfolio with a mix of stocks, bonds, mutual funds, and ETFs, then a downturn in one sector may be offset by gains in another.

» Diversification can help to maximize returns.

For example, if you invest all your money into one sector, you may miss out on growth opportunities in other sectors. By diversifying, you increase your chances of investing in top-performing asset classes.

There are several ways to diversify your investments. You can invest in different asset classes, such as stocks, bonds, and commodities. You can also invest in different sectors, such as technology, healthcare, and energy. Additionally, you can diversify by investing in different geographic regions, such as Canada, the United States, and emerging markets.

In conclusion, diversification is an essential component of a successful investment strategy. By not putting all your eggs in one basket and spreading out your investments, you can reduce risk, maximize returns, and achieve greater peace of mind.

WHAT'S THE BEST WAY TO SAVE AND INVEST?

Planning for your financial future as a teenager can be tough. Still, you should start thinking about long- and short-term savings and investments now. You might feel overwhelmed at this point and wonder, "should I invest in bonds or open an IRA?" But don't worry, the starting point is much simpler.

Remember! The first step is to start saving as soon as possible, even if it's just $5 per week. This will get you into the habit of saving money and give you time to learn about investing before making any big decisions on where or how much money should be invested.

First, let's talk about having short-term savings goals. These are typically things you want to achieve within the next few months to a year. Maybe you want to buy a new video game console, save up for a summer vacation, or even just build an emergency fund. To start, figure out how much money you'll need to save and how long it will take you to reach your goal. Then, create a budget that includes your income and expenses, and set aside a portion of your income each month towards your short-term savings goals.

Now, let's shift our focus to your long-term savings and investment goals. You want to achieve these things over several years, like saving up for college or even buying your first car or house. When it comes to long-term savings and investing, time is your friend. The earlier you start, the more time your money has to grow.

If you choose to invest your money in long-term goals, one way to do it is through a 401k or IRA account. Another option for long-term investing is the stock market. While it can be risky, investing in stocks has the potential to earn you a higher return on your investment over time. Research different companies and industries, and consider diversifying your portfolio by investing in a mix of stocks and other investments.

Lastly, remember that it is important to regularly review and adjust your savings and investment plans as your goals and financial situation change. Building wealth takes time and patience, but with a little planning and discipline, you can make sure you're financially secure.

SAVING AND INVESTING RESOURCES

It can be challenging to begin your investing and saving journey. Fortunately, there are many online tools and apps available that can make it easier. Here are four of the best online tools and apps for saving and investing:

» Acorns: This app allows you to invest your spare change automatically. When you make a purchase with a linked credit or debit card, Acorns rounds up to the nearest dollar and invests the difference in a portfolio of exchange-traded funds (ETFs). The app also offers features like recurring investments, bonus investments from certain retailers, and personalized investment advice.

» Betterment: This online investment platform uses advanced technology to help you make smart investment decisions. The app offers a range of investment options, including ETFs and mutual funds. It allows you to set up automatic contributions and rebalancing. Betterment also offers personalized financial advice and goal tracking to help you stay on track.

» Robinhood: This is an online brokerage that allows you to trade stocks, ETFs, options, and cryptocurrencies with zero commissions. The app is designed to be user-friendly and offers features like real-time market data, customizable news feeds, and a range of investment research tools. Robinhood also offers a cash management account that allows you to earn interest on your uninvested cash.

» Wealthfront: This online investment advisor uses sophisticated algorithms to manage your portfolio automatically. The app offers a range of investment options, including ETFs and individual stocks. It allows you to set up automatic contributions and rebalancing. Wealthfront also offers personalized financial advice, tax optimization strategies, and a range of other features to help you reach your investment goals.

Download these apps and see which option works best for you!

Get to work!

Once you complete these simple activities, you'll be surprised at how much you've learned about saving and investing. You're about to become a master of finance.

IN THIS ACTIVITY, YOU'LL HAVE THE CHANCE TO PRACTICE YOUR INVESTMENT SKILLS BY DECIDING WHICH OPTION BEST FITS EACH SITUATION.

Your friend's dad is starting a new business selling homemade ice cream. It's a risky venture, but it has the potential to make a lot of money.

Your grandma gave you a gift of $100 for your birthday. You want to save it for college, but you want to earn a little interest on it.

You've been working a part-time job and saving up some money. You want to invest it in something that will grow over time but don't want to pay taxes on the earnings.

You want to invest in the stock market, but you don't have enough money to buy shares in lots of different companies.

You have some money to invest, and you want to diversify your portfolio.

THE 7 STEPS TO FINANCIAL INDEPENDENCE

IT IS NEVER TOO EARLY TO START INVESTING, AND WITH THE RIGHT STRATEGIES AND MINDSET, YOU CAN ACHIEVE YOUR FINANCIAL GOALS. HERE ARE SEVEN STEPS TO HELP YOU GET STARTED.

① Decide how much to invest

Determine how much money you can afford to invest each month. This amount will vary depending on your income and expenses. It is important to have a budget to ensure you are not overspending.

 Now that you know how, create a monthly budget plan and identify how much you can allocate towards investments. You can go back to chapter 2 if you need to refresh you knowledge!

② Choosing investments

There are many types of investments to choose from, including stocks, bonds, and real estate. It is important to research and understand each type of investment before making a decision.

 Go back to the chapter and compare different types of investments. Identify the advantages and disadvantages of each type.

③ Let the snowball build

Consistency is key in investing. Make regular investments over time to allow your portfolio to grow. Remember that every little bit counts.

 Start a small investment portfolio and make regular investments over time. Track your progress and see how your portfolio grows.

④ Creating income streams

Building additional sources of income can help you achieve financial independence faster. This can include starting a side hustle or investing in dividend-paying stocks. If you don't know how to do this, don't worry! Next chapter will give you all the tools you need to succeed.

 Brainstorm ideas for creating additional sources of income. Identify ways to turn your hobbies or passions into a side hustle.

⑤ Watch your spending

It is important to keep an eye on your spending habits to ensure that you are not overspending.

 If you need to, go back to chapter 2 and identify your spending habits. You can then create a plan to manage your money better. Consider ways to reduce your expenses.

⑥ Increase your investment over time

As your income increases, consider increasing your investments to accelerate your path to financial independence.

 Set a goal to increase your investment amount over time. Identify ways to earn more income to make this possible.

⑦ Live off your investments

Once you have built a substantial investment portfolio, you may be able to live off the income generated by your investments.

 Imagine a future where you are financially independent. What would your life look like? What's the first step you need to take to get there.

Investing is a powerful tool for achieving financial independence. Following these seven steps, you can create a solid investment strategy to help you reach your financial goals. Remember to start early, be consistent, and always keep learning.

CHAPTER 3

Key takeaways

» Saving involves setting aside money that you won't spend now for emergencies or future purchases. Financial institutions offer different savings options, such as savings accounts, checking accounts, and certificates of deposit.

» Investing involves purchasing assets, like stocks or mutual funds, with the expectation of making money. Investments are selected for achieving long-term goals and can be categorized as income or growth investments. Investing has a greater risk of losing money but also has the potential to earn more money.

» Saving is suitable for short-term goals, while investing is useful for bigger financial goals that take longer to achieve. Saving and investing play a crucial role in financial well-being and can help in emergencies, such as job loss, medical emergencies, or car repairs.

» There are lots of benefits of saving and investing, such as achieve financial goals, afford big-ticket items like a car or a home. Build an emergency fund for unexpected expenses.

» There are different types of saving accounts, regular savings accounts that are safe and reliable way to store money, high-yield savings accounts, they offer higher interest rates, available through online banks, fewer fees, and many more such as, money market accounts, certificate of deposit (CD) accounts, individual retirement accounts (IRAs), health savings accounts (HSAs)

» To choose the right saving account you need to consider personal needs and situation.

» Investing involves working for money or having your money work for you. Understanding the risk-return relationship is essential in investing. Investments come in various forms, each with its own risks and potential rewards.

» Diversification is an essential strategy to reduce risk in investing. Risk tolerance refers to how comfortable you are with the possibility of losing some of your money in order to potentially gain more in the long run. Risk capacity refers to how much financial wiggle room you have when it comes to investing. Stocks and bonds are common investment vehicles, and each has its own risks and potential rewards. Tax-Free Savings Accounts (TFSAs), mutual funds, and exchange-traded funds (ETFs) are other investment vehicles to consider.

Chapter 4

Earning Money

"The only way to do great work is to love what you do. If you haven't found it yet, keep looking. Don't settle. As with all matters of the heart, you'll know when you find it."
 Steve Jobs

 **AS A TEENAGER, YOU CAN (AND SHOULD!) START THINKING ABOUT EARNING MONEY. MAKING YOUR OWN MONEY HAS MANY BENEFITS, LIKE MAKING YOU CAPABLE OF DOING THINGS INDEPENDENTLY AND PREPARING FOR THE FUTURE.**

Peter Parker, also known as Spider-Man, knows this well enough. He started a small business as a freelance photographer for the Daily Bugle (a famous New York's newspaper). This allows him to earn some extra money while also developing his skills and building his future. Just like this superhero, you can achieve your dreams by working hard.

A way of earning money as a teenager is finding something you enjoy and turning it into a profitable venture, just as Peter did. It doesn't have to be complicated; you can start your own small business with a bit of creativity and determination. You could sell handmade crafts or tutor other students. There are countless opportunities out there waiting for you.

And the Internet is an ally in our earning process. Digital life is making earning money easier than ever. Social media has revolutionized how we do business, making it easier for small businesses to thrive and for individuals to find work. You can even find job postings online and apply from the comfort of your own home! Working from home is totally a thing now, and it's not going anywhere!

This chapter will explore the ins and outs of earning money as a teenager. You'll learn how to identify your skills and interests, develop interview skills, and more. We'll also cover some common pitfalls to avoid and offer tips for staying motivated in this process.

Remember, just like Parker, you have the power to make your dreams a reality just by working and earning some money. By taking the first step towards earning money and building your financial future, you're already on your way to success. So, let's get started!

IT ALL STARTS WITH THE RIGHT SPIRIT

Maybe you understand the theory about how to start earning money, but you still don't know if you have what it takes to do it. Have you wondered what an entrepreneur is? Are you curious about what it takes to be one? Do you dream of making a name for yourself and building something from scratch? You might know names like Steve Jobs or Bill Gates.

THE ENTREPRENEUR SPIRIT

Whether you have a product idea, a passion project, or simply a desire to learn and make money, read on to discover the exciting possibilities of entrepreneurship!

Reid Hoffman, the co-founder of LinkedIn, defined an entrepreneur as "someone who jumps off a cliff and builds a plane on the way down." It's an excellent metaphor for what it takes to be an entrepreneur.

Entrepreneurship can be cool and make you feel good, but not everyone is cut out for it. It requires a ton of effort, focuses, and bravery to make it as an entrepreneur. As a teenager, you might not have much business experience yet, but that doesn't mean you can't start considering entrepreneurship as a career option.

Maddie Rae is a total boss in slime-making and a great example of a successful kid entrepreneur. Her journey began in 2017 when she, as an avid slime fan, found it hard to find slime glue in stores. Maddie decided to take matters into her own hands and worked with her dad to create their own optimized glue for slime production.

The glue was a hit, and Maddie expanded her online store to include a range of slime, glue, and accessories. Her hard work and dedication paid off; she even broke world records for slime-making and held her own conference called "Slime Bash"!

Maddie's creativity and passion for slime-making has earned her global recognition, and she's become an influencer on social media platforms. Maddie's success shows us that it's possible to turn your passion into a thriving business, no matter how young you are.

So, what does it mean to "jump off a cliff and build a plane on the way down"? In other words, it's about taking risks, trying new things, and being willing to fail. Entrepreneurs don't always have a clear plan or roadmap to success. Instead, they're constantly experimenting, iterating, and adapting.

One of the first steps in becoming an entrepreneur is identifying what kind of business you want to start. Different types of entrepreneurs exist, such as buyers, imitators, innovators, hustlers, researchers, financiers, and prodigies. Each type of entrepreneurship requires other skills and approaches.

ENTREPRENEUR TYPES[1]

There are many kinds of entrepreneurs, each with unique qualities and ways of doing things. This means that no two entrepreneurs are precisely the same!

First up, we have buyers. They are entrepreneurs who purchase existing businesses and run them to make them more profitable. They have been there, done that, and have deep pockets to show for it. They typically have experience running a successful business. They are now looking to expand their portfolio with new and original opportunities.

Another type of entrepreneur is the imitator. They mimic successful business models and adapt them to their own markets. Imitators take what is already working, make it more appealing (through innovation or iteration), and build a product or service around it. Mark Zuckerberg can be a great example of this. The network he created was different but based on ideas that had already been explored.

Innovators create something new or improve an existing product or service. As noted by Forbes, they have creative minds and enjoy developing new ideas. Alphabet Inc.'s (Google) co-founder and CEO, Larry Page, is an innovator. This company develops products and services in the internet, software, electronic devices, and other technologies. In addition to being creative, Larry founded an innovative company.

Hustlers are entrepreneurs who are quick on their feet and always looking for ways to grow their businesses. They use their skills to identify and exploit new opportunities. They dream big (sometimes ridiculously so), aren't afraid to take risks and work hard every day to make those dreams a reality.

 Researchers spend a lot of time studying their industry and market. They use data and analysis to identify trends and make informed business decisions.

 Financiers are entrepreneurs who provide funding for new businesses. They invest in promising startups and help them get off the ground.

 Lastly, we have prodigies. These entrepreneurs start their own businesses at a young age and have a natural talent for entrepreneurship. Steve Jobs is an excellent example of a prodigy. Isn't it amazing to think that his journey began in his garage? Since childhood, he excelled at everything he did, and built what is now one of our most successful companies from scratch.

Entrepreneurs are some of the most driven, passionate, and hardworking people. They come in all shapes and sizes, but they all have one thing in common: the desire to succeed.

From Steve Jobs and Bill Gates to everyday folks like you and me, entrepreneurs are all around us, and their stories are truly awe-inspiring. In fact, history is full of people who exemplify the entrepreneurial spirit and have achieved great things.

Bill Gates
MICROSOFT FOUNDER

Gates knew the value of being your own boss and controlling your destiny. And he started early: at just 13 years old! Even at such a young age, he was already working with computers and building the foundation for a groundbreaking career.

But it wasn't just about getting started early - Gates also believed in the importance of quality and presentation. As he famously said, "If you can't make it good, at least make it look good." So whether you're starting a new business, pursuing a passion project, or just trying to get ahead in life, remember the lessons of Bill Gates and never stop striving for excellence.

Mark Zuckerberg
FACEBOOK FOUNDER

As he famously said, "The biggest risk is not taking any risk… In a world that is changing really quickly, the only strategy that is guaranteed to fail is not taking risks." And boy, did he take risks - he started Facebook in his college dorm room and turned it into one of the biggest companies in the world. But it wasn't just about making a name for himself - Zuckerberg also believed in the power of connection and bringing people together. That's why Facebook has become such an integral part of our lives, from staying in touch with friends and family to connecting with people worldwide.

HOW TO BECOME AN ENTREPRENEUR AS A TEENAGER

Becoming an entrepreneur is all about identifying a need in the market and coming up with a unique solution. This means being very wise in reading what people around you need and giving them an answer. It's about being creative, taking risks, and being passionate about what you do.

Think about what you're passionate about or what problems you want to solve. Do you have a talent or skill that you can monetize? Is there something you wish existed, but can't find it anywhere? These could be the seeds of a business idea.

Being an entrepreneur is about more than just making money. It's about having a vision and purpose and using your business to positively impact the world. You can be an agent of change, whether it's in your community or beyond.

Becoming an entrepreneur as a teenager is all about taking action and trying new things. Don't be afraid to fail; every failure is a learning opportunity.

SIMPLE STEPS TO BECOMING A YOUNG ENTREPRENEUR

1. Identify your passion: Think about what you love doing and how you can turn it into a business. Passion is the key to success as an entrepreneur.
2. Start small: Try to tackle only a little at a time. Start with a small project and grow from there.
3. Read motivational books: books that encourage you and give you ideas are a great way to start to get in the entrepreneur field.
4. Be persistent: Entrepreneurship is not easy, and there will be challenges along the way. Be persistent and keep pushing forward.
5. Learn from failure: Failure is a part of entrepreneurship. Use it as an opportunity to learn and grow.
6. Stay organized: Being organized is essential to running a successful business. Keep track of your finances, schedules, and deadlines.

Now that you know how to become an entrepreneur as a teenager, let's discuss some ways to make money. Becoming an entrepreneur is just one way to earn money, but many simple options might suit you better.

Whether you're saving up for college, looking to buy a car, or just wanting to have some extra cash in your pocket, teenagers have plenty of opportunities to earn money. So, let's explore some of them!

WAYS TO EARN MONEY AS A TEENAGER

As a teenager, there are thousands of ways to make money. All you have to do is be open and ready to seize the opportunities that come your way. But if you need help coming up with ideas, don't worry!

Earning money as a teenager is not just about making some extra cash. It's also an opportunity to gain work experience, develop important skills, and learn the value of money. Start exploring the suitable options for you and start on the road to financial independence.

HOW TO KNOW THE RIGHT FIT FOR YOU

To figure out what kind of work might be the best fit for you, start by asking yourself some key questions.

¿How much time do I have available?

_____

¿What is something I am good at?

_____

¿How much money do I plan on making?

_____

Ultimately, finding the right job is about aligning your strengths, interests, time, and financial needs. By asking yourself these questions and exploring your options, you'll be well on your way to finding the perfect fit for you.

Ideas

If you're struggling to come up with ideas or feeling unsure about what to do, consider this guide to help get you started.

BABYSIT

Offer to watch your younger siblings or cousins, or even post on social media to find families needing a babysitter.

WALKING DOGS

Check with your neighbors or post flyers around your neighborhood offering to walk their dogs for a fee.

WASH CARS

Offer to wash cars for neighbors or family members for a fee, and expand your business by offering detailing services too!

SELLING T-SHIRTS

Create your own designs and sell them online or at local markets or events.

TAKE SURVEYS ONLINE

You can find paid surveys that are easy and don't consume much time.

YARD SALE

Clean out your closet and sell your gently used clothes, electronics, or toys at a yard sale or online.

GIVE MUSIC LESSONS

If you're musically talented, offer to teach beginners or younger kids how to play an instrument.

MAKE YOUTUBE VIDEOS

Start a YouTube channel on a topic that interests you, like gaming or beauty, and earn money from ads once you have a following.

MAKE AND SELL CRAFTS

If you're crafty, make and sell your creations online or at local craft fairs.

HOUSEHOLD CHORES

Offer to help your family with chores like cleaning, laundry, or cooking for a fee.

Remember, these informal jobs are a great way to get started and gain some experience, but if you're looking for something more stable and long-term, you may want to consider applying for a part-time job. Many places hire teenagers, such as grocery stores, restaurants, and retail shops. You can check online job boards or even visit local establishments to see if they are hiring. Applying for a job can be a breeze when you have the right information.

JOB APPLICATION 101: WHAT YOU NEED TO KNOW

Getting an informal job can be a great way to start your career. It can help you develop essential skills such as responsibility and time management. But if you want to take things one step forward, maybe a part-time job is what you're looking for. Not only can this provide you with a steady paycheck, but it can also give you valuable experience in the workforce that you can use in the future. Plus, you might even discover a new passion or interest through your job!

It's not impossible to apply for a first job, but here are a few tips you might find helpful.

PREPARING A RESUME

Your resume is your ticket to your dream job, and it's essential to make it stand out. It is basically a document that tells your future boss all about your past experiences, skills, and work history. It's a chance to show off what makes you unique and why you're the perfect fit for the job. With some guidance, you can create a winning resume highlighting your strengths and standing out from the competition.

The first thing you need to do is identify the skills and experiences that you want to highlight. Are you a great team player? Do you have excellent organizational skills? Are you a natural-born leader? Whatever your strengths are, make sure to put them front and center.

Next up, let's talk about formatting. You want to ensure your resume is clear and easy to read. Start with your personal information, followed by your studies, skills, and experience. And don't forget to use bullet points to make everything nice and organized.

Last but not least, proofread, proofread, proofread! Make sure there are no typos or grammatical errors. And don't forget to tailor your resume to the job you're applying for. You want to ensure that your resume shows how your skills and experiences align with what the employer is looking for.

 Finding the perfect template for your resume can be a daunting task. Still, thankfully there are many resources available to help you out. One of the best places to start is online, where you can find a wide range of high-quality resume templates specifically designed to help you showcase your skills and experiences in the best possible light.

One website that you may find particularly helpful is https://resume.io/resume-templates. For professional easy-to-follow templates, Canva is also a fantastic free option. Here, you can find a vast array of customizable templates tailored to suit various industries and job roles. These templates are user-friendly, easy to navigate, and offer a range of options to help you create a professional-looking resume that will impress potential employers.

The benefit of using a template is that it provides a solid foundation for you to build upon, allowing you to focus on highlighting your skills and experiences rather than worrying about the layout and design of your resume. With a well-designed template, you can rest assured that your resume will be structured clearly and concisely, making it easy for hiring managers to quickly identify your strengths and qualifications.

Once your resume is ready, apply for your first job!

APPLYING FOR A JOB

The next step is to send your resume to different places and apply for various jobs once you have completed your resume. This might seem simple, but you should have some steps in mind to succeed.

1. START BY RESEARCHING THE COMPANY AND JOB REQUIREMENTS.

If you're looking for a job, researching the company and job requirements is an essential step before submitting your resume. Doing so can help you tailor your application to meet the company's specific needs and increase your chances of being selected for the job.

To start, visit the company's website and read its mission statement, core values, and any other relevant information that can give you an idea of its culture and what they stand for. You can also check the company's social media pages and read their posts, reviews, and comments to see what customers and employees say about them. Additionally, thoroughly research the job requirements to ensure that you meet the qualifications and skills required for the position. Look at the job posting and identify the required skills, experience, and education.

2. WRITE A COVER LETTER THAT SHOWCASES WHY YOU'RE A GOOD FIT FOR THE POSITION.

After you have conducted research on the company and job requirements, the next step is to create a compelling cover letter that showcases why you are the best fit for the position. A cover letter is an opportunity to introduce yourself, highlight your relevant skills and experiences, and demonstrate your enthusiasm for the role.

» The first paragraph of your cover letter should introduce yourself and explain your interest in the position.

» The second paragraph is where you can highlight your relevant skills and experiences. Use concrete examples to demonstrate your qualifications, such as specific projects you have worked on or achievements you have earned in previous roles.

» The third paragraph is where you can show your enthusiasm for the role and the company. Highlight what you find exciting about the position and the company and why you are motivated to work for them. You can mention any research you have done on the company culture or recent projects they have undertaken to show that you are truly interested in the company beyond just the job opening.

» Finally, close your cover letter by thanking the hiring manager for their time and consideration, and mention that you would be happy to discuss your qualifications further in an interview. Provide your contact information, such as your email and phone number, so that they can reach out to you easily.

Suppose you've successfully applied for a job and landed an interview. In that case, it's time to showcase your skills and abilities to the employer. This is your opportunity to make a lasting impression and prove why you're the best candidate for the job.

DEVELOPING INTERVIEW SKILLS

» Practicing common interview questions and responses.

As a teenager, you may feel nervous about attending a job interview. One way to help ease your nerves is to practice common interview questions and responses beforehand. Start by researching common questions often asked in interviews and prepare your answers. You can also practice with a friend or family member or record yourself answering the questions to see how you come across. Practicing can help you feel more confident and prepared for the interview, making it easier to answer questions clearly and confidently.

» Dressing appropriately and arriving early to the interview
First impressions are important, and the way you present yourself can have a big impact on how you are perceived in an interview. As a teenager, it's essential to dress appropriately and arrive early to the interview. Choose a professional and neat outfit, avoiding clothing that is too casual or revealing. Ensure your clothes are clean and ironed, and avoid wearing too much jewelry or accessories. Arrive at the interview location at least 15 minutes early to give yourself enough time to check in and prepare. Being punctual and well-dressed shows you are serious about the job and value the interviewer's time.

» Demonstrating confidence and enthusiasm for the job
During the interview, it's important to demonstrate confidence and enthusiasm. Speak clearly and confidently, making eye contact with the interviewer. Show your enthusiasm for the job by highlighting why you are interested in the position and what you find exciting about the company. Be sure to mention any relevant experience or skills that make you a good fit for the job. Confidence comes from being prepared, so practice your responses beforehand and research the company and job requirements. Demonstrating confidence and enthusiasm can help you stand out from other candidates and increase your chances of being selected for the job.

As you can see, there's more to personal finances than just numbers and banks. Understanding money is also about learning about yourself, who you are, and your unique talents and abilities. When you know your own values and strengths, you can use money to create the life you want and positively impact the world around you. Whether you're looking to start your own business, take on an informal job, or apply for your first part-time job, the world is full of opportunities waiting for you to seize them. Remember to always stay true to your passions and interests, stay curious and open-minded, and never stop learning. With hard work, dedication, and a little creativity, you'll be on your way to success in no time. Don't let anything hold you back from pursuing your dreams!

Activity 1:

MAKE YOUR OWN BUSINESS PLAN.

Fill out this business plan to begin projecting how you will start your entrepreneur road. Read the questions in each box. Add your timetable to fit your project into your routine.

KID'S BUSINESS PLAN

What do you want to sell?

_____   _____
_____   _____
_____   _____

Final choice:

_____

What do you want to call your business?

_____   _____
_____   _____

Final choice:

_____

Where are you going to do it?

_____   _____
_____   _____
_____   _____

Final choice:

_____

How are you going to be organizing your time?

_____

_____

_____

In here, you write all the activities of the week

In here, you write your times	Monday	Tuesday	Wednesday	Thursday	Friday

Activity 2:

CREATE YOUR FIRST RESUME.

Create your own resume by adding your personal information in the blank spaces.

Here is an example so you can learn how to do it:

EMMA JACKSON

TEENAGER WITH LEADERSHIP SKILLS AND CAPABLE OF WORKING WITH A TEAM

CONTACT

📍 Cerritos, California

✉ emma@gmail.com

📞 (555) 555-1234

EDUCATION

Whitney High School
City Cerritos
Start:
August 2021 - present

EMPLOYMENT

Babysitter: I have watched babies since young age and enjoy being with kids all my life. I can manage crying and pressure.

SKILLS

Leadership

Teamwork

Creativity

LANGUAGES

English

Spanish

HOBBIES

Painting
Singing
Reading

NAME:

DESCRIPTION:

Add a pic of
yourself here

CONTACT

SKILLS

EDUCATION

LANGUAGES

EMPLOYMENT

HOBBIES

CHAPTER 4

Key takeaways

» There are thousands of ways for you to make money - all you have to do is be open and ready to seize the opportunities that come your way

» Being an entrepreneur can be really cool and make you feel good, but not everyone is cut out for it. It requires a ton of effort, focus, and bravery to make it as an entrepreneur.

» There are lots of different types of entrepreneurs, each with their own special qualities and ways of doing things. You have the buyers, who purchase existing businesses and run them to make them more profitable. The imitators who mimic successful business, the innovators that are the ones who think outside of the box and create things that are new. Hustlers are entrepreneurs who are quick on their feet and always looking for ways to grow their businesses. Researchers spend a lot of time studying their industry and market. Financiers are entrepreneurs who provide funding for new businesses, and prodigies that have a natural talent for entrepreneurship.

» Examples of entrepreneurs are Bill Gates and Mark Zuckerberg, who show that having a great idea, enthusiasm and working hard is key in this process.

» Some ideas to earn some money could be, babysit, a yard sale, walking dogs, give music lessons, sell t-shirts, wash cars and lots more.

» A resume tells the employer about your experiences, skills and work history. To make it you have to identify the skills and experiences that you want to highlight, write it and PROOFREAD.

» Applying for a job is not hard, it is all about researching the company and job requirements, writing a cover letter that showcases why you're a good fit for the position and waiting for a response.

» Interview skills are really important because it helps to communicate correctly with the company. You can start by practicing common interview questions and responses to be good at this point.

1   The 10 types of entrepreneurs and why you need to know them. Bond Collective. (n.d.). Retrieved March 27, 2023, from https://www.bondcollective.com/blog/types-of-entrepreneurs/

Chapter 5

Smart shopping

"Money is not everything, but when you start thinking about rent and car payments, it becomes everything."
Cardi B

HAVE YOU EVER FELT LIKE YOUR MONEY IS A SLIPPERY FISH THAT WRIGGLES OUT OF YOUR GRASP? IT'S LIKE TRYING TO HOLD ONTO A HANDFUL OF WATER. THE HARDER YOU TRY, THE MORE IT SLIPS AWAY.

In the movie "Confessions of a Shopaholic," we see the consequences of letting our spending habits spiral out of control. Rebecca Bloomwood's fashion addiction leads her down a dangerous path of overspending and debt.

Just like Rebeca Bloom showed us, earning money is not enough. We also need to spend it wisely. This movie portrays the consequences of irresponsible spending and the importance of making informed purchasing decisions. How many times have you been Rebeca Bloom?

Even though you may need to buy things, it is not always the best decision. When making the most out of the money you've earned, being thoughtful about your purchases is crucial. Without any control or limit, you'll probably waste all your money without noticing. Before spending your money, planning how you will organize your spending is essential.

Today we are bombarded with more advertisements and publicity than we even realize, and we gradually believe that we need certain things that we don't. The more you understand this marketing world, the more you'll be able to discover the messages behind a publicity campaign.

Throughout this chapter, you will learn how to spend your money intelligently and mindfully, understand what sales and promotions mean, and get a taste of online shopping. So let's start this shopping trip through chapter 5!

HOW SMART SHOPPING CAN SAVE YOU MONEY

Smart shopping is all about buying things you need and being thoughtful with your spending. If you make $400 a week and spend all your money on Starbucks, new nikes, clothes, and eating out, you are not managing your money correctly.

As a teenager, it can be tempting to buy things impulsively without considering the consequences. You may feel pressure to keep up with your peers or always need the latest gadgets and trends. If you buy things uncontrollably, you're likely to develop negative traits that aren't good for anyone, especially someone just beginning to establish good financial habits.

Impulse shopping is a common habit among teenagers that can lead to overspending and unnecessary clutter. When you buy things without analyzing your purchases, you may end up with items you don't need or want, which can take up valuable space in your home and cause unnecessary stress. Additionally, impulse buying can lead to overspending, quickly depleting your savings and leaving you financially difficult.

Also, overspending is another negative trait resulting from buying things uncontrollably. As a teenager, you may not have a lot of financial responsibilities, but overspending can still have long-term consequences. When you consistently spend more than you can afford, it can set a dangerous precedent for your financial habits in the future.

BENEFITS OF SMART SHOPPING

In purchasing things smartly, the most significant change you'll notice is how much money you save. Taking a step back and analyzing your spending habits is one of the best ways to save money.

When you take time to think about what you spend your money on, you can make more informed purchasing decisions. This, in turn, leads you to purchase fewer things that you don't need and ultimately save more money in the long run. Suppose you analyze your monthly expenses and identify areas to cut back. In that case, you can redirect that money toward other important goals, such as investing or retirement savings.

Also, today's world is constantly bombarded with advertisements and marketing tactics that try to persuade you to buy certain products. People who buy impulsively usually fall for more scams than those who take the time to make intelligent purchases.

As not all products are created equal, it's important to distinguish genuine value from scams. Shopping smart, especially when purchasing clothing, can help you avoid scams. You should research before buying a product, read reviews, and only purchase from reputable retailers.

But also, smart shopping can make you grateful for what you already have. Buying in a mindful way helps you appreciate what you have before creating new needs. By appreciating what you have, you are less likely to feel the need to constantly buy new things to replace or upgrade what you already have. For example, instead of buying a new phone every year, you'll focus on taking care of the one you have, making it last longer.

You need to start being thoughtful about purchases to reap all the benefits smart shopping brings.

SMART SHOPPING 101: MAKING INFORMED PURCHASES

An essential first step in smart shopping is analyzing what we want to purchase. Buying something is not as simple as you might think, and research and evaluation are important when deciding what to buy. Here are some key steps you can follow to be sure you're making the best buying decision.

EVALUATING PRODUCT REVIEWS AND RATINGS

When you're in the market for a specific product, the first thing to do is research. Look for information about the product and read reviews from other customers who have purchased it. This can give you an idea of the quality of the product, how well it works, and any potential drawbacks or issues to consider. Additionally, researching the product can help you identify any possible scams or fraudulent products you may want to avoid.

RESEARCHING PRODUCTS AND COMPARING PRICES

Once you've narrowed down your options and found a product that meets your needs, the next step is to compare prices. Don't settle for the first price you see! Take the time to shop around and compare prices from different retailers. You may be surprised that prices can vary significantly from one store to another, even for the same product. Compare prices to ensure you get the best deal and maximize your budget.

CONSIDERING THE OVERALL VALUE AND LONG-TERM USE OF A PRODUCT

As a teenager, it can be tempting to choose products based on what's trendy without giving much thought to their overall value or long-term use. However, considering a product's overall value and long-term use is important to remember.

When considering a product's value, think about how well it will meet your needs and how long it will last. For example, buying a cheaper version of a product may seem like a good idea in the short term. Still, if it breaks or wears out quickly, you may have to replace it sooner than you would if you had invested in a higher-quality product. Additionally, when you choose a product that meets your needs and lasts a long time, you can save money in the long run by avoiding the need to replace it frequently.

Danger!
Avoiding impulse buys

Avoiding impulse purchases is the second step towards living a more thoughtful shopping life. You buy on impulse when you don't think about it first, but here's some advice you can follow to stop yourself from buying without thinking.

IDENTIFY TRIGGERS THAT LEAD TO IMPULSE BUYING

It can be challenging to resist the urge to make impulse purchases, but identifying the triggers that lead to these purchases can help you take control of your spending. Many things can trigger an impulse buy, including the constant barrage of advertising we're exposed to daily, shopping apps on our phones, and even the simple act of going to the mall.

» Social media advertisement: There are many platforms, such as Instagram, that are full of ads that are carefully targeted to appeal to your interests, making it all too easy to click through and make a purchase without even thinking twice. If you find yourself making impulsive purchases after scrolling through your social media feed, try taking a break from these platforms or unfollowing accounts that tend to promote products heavily.

» Going to the mall or shopping center: being surrounded by various products can be overwhelming, and it's easy to get caught up in the excitement of the shopping experience. You can set a time limit for your shopping trip to help you stay focused and avoid getting sidetracked by things you don't need.

» Shopping apps: These apps make purchasing incredibly easy with just a few taps. They often use notifications and other tactics to encourage you to make more purchases. If you make impulsive purchases through these apps, try deleting them from your phone or disabling notifications, so you're not constantly bombarded with reminders to buy things.

USE SHOPPING LISTS AND STICK TO A BUDGET
You can prevent impulse buys by making a list of what you need before shopping and sticking to it until you have everything you need. It can also be helpful to have a budget in place.

The problem with shopping without a limit is that you will be easily influenced and will be led to buy things that you don't actually need if you go without any limits.

WAIT 24 HOURS BEFORE MAKING A PURCHASE TO THINK IT OVER
We all know the feeling of seeing something we want to buy, but sometimes it's not always the best idea to make an impulse purchase. That's where the 24-hour rule comes in!

Here's how it works: if you need to decide whether to buy something, wait to purchase it. Instead, wait 24 hours before making a decision. During that time, consider whether you need the item and whether it's worth the money you'd spend on it. After 24 hours, if you still want the item and feel like you need it, go ahead and buy it. But if you've forgotten about it or no longer feel like you need it, it's best to leave it and wait for something better.

Next time you're tempted to make an impulse purchase, try waiting 24 hours and see how you feel. You might be surprised at how much money you can save and how much better you'll feel knowing that you've made a thoughtful, deliberate decision about your spending.

Identifying triggers and avoiding impulse shopping are essential parts of shopping smartly, but those aren't the only things. Being mindful about your spending also means knowing how much you can afford to spend and when is the best time to purchase. Taking advantage of sales and promotions is tempting, but planning ahead can help you get the most out of them.

UNDERSTANDING
SALES AND PROMOTIONS

If you love to shop, you've probably noticed that sales and promotions can be a great way to save money and score some awesome deals. But it's essential to be smart about sales and promotions so that you don't spend more money than you intended.

GOOD DEAL OR A MARKETING PLOY?

Some sales and promotions can make us think that buying more is better or that we suddenly need something we never even thought about before. Recognizing the difference between a good deal and a marketing ploy is important.

So, how can you tell if a sale or promotion is really a good deal? One way is to ask yourself a few critical questions before purchasing. For example,

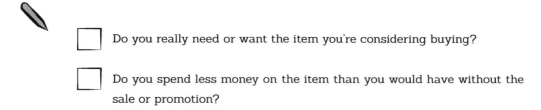

☐ Do you really need or want the item you're considering buying?

☐ Do you spend less money on the item than you would have without the sale or promotion?

If the answer to both of these questions is yes, then it's likely that you've found a good deal.

But what about when a sale or promotion seems too good to be true? Doing a little research before making a purchase is always a good idea, especially if you need to figure out whether the deal is worth it. Plenty of resources are available online to help you compare prices and read reviews from other customers.

 One excellent resource is ConsumerReports.org, which provides unbiased reviews of products and services.

SOMETIMES YOU HAVE TO BE FAST

Impulse buying can damage your economy. Still, sometimes you have to act fast, which does not mean buying impulsively. Remember that sales and promotions often have a time limit, so it's essential to act fast to take advantage of a special deal.

For example, you might see a sale for 50% off all clothes at your favorite store, but the sale might only last for one day. If you wait too long, you might miss the opportunity to save some serious cash.

Planning ahead to make the most out of sales time is essential. You can write down a list of what you need to purchase and the budget you'll devote to those things.

PROMOTIONS AND DISCOUNTS: UNDERSTAND THE TERMS.

It's essential to read the fine print and understand the terms and conditions before making a purchase. For instance, some promotions may come with limitations or exclusions that may not be immediately apparent. These can include restrictions on certain products, minimum purchase amounts, or specific dates and times when the discount can be applied. By understanding these terms and conditions, you can avoid disappointment and make the most of the promotion.

It's also important to remember that promotions and discounts may have expiration dates or limited quantities available.

Reading and understanding the terms and conditions of promotions and discounts can help you make smarter purchasing decisions. You can also find more information and tips on how to shop smartly by visiting reputable online sources, such as consumer advocacy websites and financial blogs.

So before making your next purchase, be sure to research and understand the details of the promotion or discount to get the most out of your shopping experience.

SHOPPING
ONLINE VS. IN-PERSON

With the digitalized world comes the convenience of online shopping, which has made buying products as easy as a few clicks. But is this shopping style actually better than in-person shopping?

Let's be honest, shopping is a fun activity, whether it's online or in-person. Both types of shopping have their positive and negative aspects, and knowing the difference between them can help you make the most out of each.

Online shopping

PRO'S	CON'S
» It's easier	» There is a lot of marketing in the middle of it, so you may be tempted to buy without need.
» There are no salespeople to pressure you.	
» You can make shopping smarter if you use it wisely.	» As it doesn't feel like "spending money" you can be tempted to make a purchase without thinking about it.

Shopping in person

PRO'S	CON'S
» It's a more mindful approach to shopping.	» The process is more tedious and slow since you have to go to the location.
» You can try on clothes.	

In-person shopping has its time and place, just as online shopping does.

When buying clothes, accessories, and shoes, in-person shopping is the best option. You can try on clothes, check the fit and color, and get advice from salespeople. This way, you can purchase mindfully, knowing you're getting something that fits and suits you.

However, online shopping is an excellent option for groceries and electronics. It saves time, and you can compare prices and products with ease. Plus, you can have everything delivered right to your doorstep, making it a convenient option for those with a busy schedule.

Remember, both online and in-person shopping have their benefits, and it's up to you to decide which method is the best for your needs.

CONSIDER SHIPPING COSTS AND DELIVERY TIMES

Regarding online shopping, it's essential to consider additional factors such as shipping costs and delivery times. While the convenience of shopping from the comfort of your own home is undeniable, these additional costs and potential delays can make a big difference in the overall value of your purchase.

Before making a purchase online, check the shipping fee and delivery times. Some retailers offer free shipping after a certain purchase threshold, so it may be worth considering adding additional items to your cart to meet that threshold. Additionally, check the expected delivery times to ensure that the item will arrive on time.

Another helpful tip is to read comments or reviews from other customers regarding their experiences with delivery. This can give you a better idea of any potential issues or delays you may encounter, and help you make a more informed decision before completing your purchase.

Remember, online shopping can be a great way to save time and find great deals. Still, it's essential to consider all the factors involved to ensure you're getting the best value for your money.

SAFETY TIPS FOR SHOPPING ONLINE

Shopping online can be convenient and hassle-free. Still, keeping some safety tips in mind is essential to avoid fraud or scams.

» Make sure to check the seller's legitimacy before making a purchase. Look for reviews and ratings of the seller or website and ensure they have a secure connection (https://) before entering personal information.

» Be wary of email scams, which often appear as promotions or offers. Don't click on links or download attachments from unknown or suspicious sources, as they could be viruses or phishing attempts

» If you suspect any fraudulent activity, immediately report it to the appropriate authorities and your bank or credit card company.

These safety tips will help you enjoy online shopping while protecting your personal info.

LET'S WORK TOGETHER ✏️
Activity 1

TOM

Tom had been saving up for months to buy a new gaming console, but when he walked into the electronics store, he was overwhelmed by all the choices. He started browsing and quickly found himself drawn to a display of flashy headphones.

Tom had never considered buying headphones before, but these were so cool looking and had all the latest features. Before he knew it, he grabbed a pair and went to the checkout counter.

A few days later, the headphones arrived in the mail, and Tom excitedly tore open the packaging. But as he tried to connect them to his phone, he realized they were incompatible. He had not checked the product specifications before making the purchase.

Frustrated and disappointed, Tom realized that he had made an impulsive decision that had cost him a lot of money. He had not thought about the long-term value of the headphones or whether he really needed them.

From that day on, Tom learned the importance of being a mindful shopper. He started researching products before purchasing and read reviews to see what others thought about the product. He also made sure to check the seller's legitimacy and used secure payment methods when shopping online.

Tom realized that impulse buying could lead to negative consequences and that it was important to consider the overall value and long-term use of a product. He was glad that he had learned this lesson early on and could now make smarter and more informed buying decisions.

» What are some important things Tom learned about impulse buying?

» Tom considers research a good idea before purchasing. What does this mean and why is it a good idea?

» Knowing how to make good spending decisions is part of building good financial habits. What are some factors that influence Tom spending decisions?

CHAPTER 5

Key takeaways

» Smart shopping is all about buying things that you need and being thoughtful with your spending. Is an important skill that can help you save money, avoid scams, and appreciate the value of what you have.

» People who buy things uncontrollably are likely to develop negative habits, especially those just beginning to develop good finances. They might be overspending, falling into debt or maybe not being able to save any money even though they work a lot.

» It is essential to analyze what we want to purchase before we begin smart shopping. The purchasing process is not as simple as we think, and research and evaluation are important when making the right purchase decision. It's important to think about whether you really need the item and whether it's worth the price. This may involve doing research, comparing prices, and evaluating the quality of the product.

» One of the biggest obstacles to smart shopping is impulse buying, which involves making a purchase without thinking it through first. Taking control of your shopping habits means avoiding impulse purchases and taking the time to consider your options.

» Sales and promotions can be a great way to save money and get good deals, but it's important to be smart about them. Avoid overspending by setting a budget and sticking to it, and be wary of deals that seem too good to be true.

» The rise of online shopping has made buying products more convenient than ever, but it can also lead to impulse buying. When shopping online, take the time to consider whether you really need the item and whether it's worth the price.

Chapter 6

Credit and Debt

"Rather go to bed without
dinner than to rise in debt."
Benjamin Franklin

WITH JUST THREE CLUES, CAN YOU GUESS WHICH DISNEY MOVIE CHARACTER I'M TALKING ABOUT?
- » **SHE'S A REDHEADED PRINCESS.**
- » **THERE ARE MANY RULES SHE LOVES TO BREAK.**
- » **SHE OWES A WITCH A HUGE DEBT.**

Perhaps the drawing above tipped you off, or maybe you're a Disney fan who guessed it based on hints, or you still don't know who I'm talking about. Either case, it was Ariel from The Little Mermaid, who you had to guess.

In this classic movie, Ariel dreams of leaving her undersea life and exploring the human world. She becomes so enamored with the human world that she makes a deal with the sea witch, Ursula, and trades her voice for a pair of legs. However, Ariel quickly learns that her deal comes with a high cost and has put herself in debt to the sea witch.

If Ariel cannot win the prince's love in that time, she will return to the sea and become the witch's property. Prompted by love and hope, Ariel accepts the deal. What a huge risk she took!

Like Ariel, you may be tempted to make impulsive decisions, such as taking on debt to buy things you want but don't necessarily need. As her experience illustrates, you can quickly get into debt and over your head, if you aren't careful with your spending.

When it comes to debt, there's more to it than just spending the right amount. Credit and debt are two sides of the same coin, and it's essential to understand how they work together. Your credit score reflects your responsibility for borrowing money and paying it back on time. Suppose you consistently make on-time payments and keep your credit utilization low. In that case, your credit score will improve, making it easier to get approved for loans and credit cards with better terms and interest rates.

On the flip side, if you take on too much debt or miss payments, your credit score will suffer, making it harder to get approved for credit in the future. This can lead to a vicious cycle of borrowing more and more just to stay afloat, which can quickly spiral out of control. Are you ready to dive into the sea of credit and debt and discover its hidden treasures? Let's go!

WHAT THE HECK IS CREDIT?

Buying on credit is all about buying now, paying later. Here's how it works: let's say you want to buy a new phone but don't have all the money right now. You could use credit to buy it! This means the store gives you the phone, and you promise to pay in the future. That is, you owe the money to your bank or the store directly (but we'll get to that!). Here's the catch: for using credit, you'll be charged a little extra. We call this interest.

So, why would you want to buy something on credit instead of waiting until you have the money saved? Well, sometimes there are things you need or want right away, like a new computer for school or a plane ticket to visit family. Credit allows you to buy things you couldn't afford otherwise. By using credit responsibly, you can build your credit history and make qualifying for loans and credit cards easier.

However, here's the key: using credit responsibly means being sure you'll be able to pay it back on time and not getting in over your head with debt. Remember, just because you can buy something on credit doesn't mean you should. Make sure you have a plan for paying it off monthly to avoid interest, and avoid using credit for things you don't really need.

TYPES OF CREDIT

Did you know there are three main types of credit? First up, there's investment credit. This is when big companies borrow a lot of money to build new factories or buy equipment. Think of it like taking out a mega loan.

Next, we have commercial credit. Businesses use short-term borrowing to get more products on their shelves before busy shopping seasons, like the holidays. So, if your favorite store wants to stock up on Halloween costumes, they might use commercial credit to buy them.

> Credit and debt are two sides of the same coin, and it's essential to understand how they work together.

Finally, there's consumer credit. You might use this kind of credit to buy stuff for yourself, like a car or a new TV. Consumer credit can be long-term, like when you take out a big loan to buy a house, or short-term, like when you use a credit card to buy a new phone.

WHAT ABOUT CREDIT CARDS?

Like fish in the sea, there are many types of credit cards. For instance, did you know many stores, especially large department stores, issue customers their branded cards? Major department stores like Macy's or Target issue them, which can only be used at that specific store.

Then, there are all-purpose cards like bank cards and travel and entertainment cards. You've probably heard of Visa and MasterCard, right? Those are bank cards. These cards are widely accepted in many countries. They can be used to pay for nearly anything, including your Spotify subscription or a new Iphone.

But there are also travel and entertainment cards, like American Express, that were originally meant for paying for plane tickets and fancy dinners but can now be used for all sorts of purchases, like clothes and electronics.

So how do credit cards actually work?

Basically, when you use a credit card to make a purchase, you'll get a bill in the mail within a month, and the amount you owe is called your "Balance." So if you sign up for that Disney+ subscription for $100, your balance goes up by $100.

But here's the thing, every credit card has a limit on how much you can owe at one time. This is called your credit limit. So, let's say you signed up for Disney+ and your balance is now $100. If your credit limit is $1,000, then your available credit would be $900. Easy peasy, right?

In any case, if you make a payment on your credit card, your available credit goes back up again. That's why credit cards are known as a revolving line of credit - you can keep using them and borrowing from them as long as you pay your bill and have credit available.

Depending on the type of credit card you've used, the store will get paid differently. For instance, a department store may issue its own bills. But if you use bank cards and travel and entertainment cards, they work differently. The card issuers (banks, for example) act as intermediaries between the seller and buyer.

Let's say you want to buy a new video game console for $300 maybe you need at the "Game Store". You use your credit card to pay for it. When the Game Store processes your payment, they send a credit slip to your card issuer. The issuer pays the seller the $300, but they also deduct a service charge, say $10. So the seller gets $290, and the credit card issuer bills you $300. Now, when it comes to paying for your credit card purchases, you've got two options:

⟶ OPTION 1:

Pay it off in full within a month. This is highly Recommended.

or

⟶ OPTION 2:

Make extended payments over some time. Note that if you take this option, you should always cover the monthly payment amount.

If you choose the second option, interest fees and carrying balance charges will be charged on top. If you go with option 2, the extended payment option, it's called a revolving account.

You'll have a maximum debt limit and need to make periodic payments based on the size of your debt.

HOW CAN YOU APPLY FOR A CREDIT CARD?

Getting a credit card is not as difficult as you might think, but there are a few things to remember.

» Age requirement: In the USA, you must be at least 18 years old to apply for a credit card on your own. If you are under 18, you may be able to become an authorized user on someone else's credit card.

» Research: Before applying for a credit card, research to find the best option for your needs. Look for cards with low or no annual fees, low-interest rates, and rewards programs that align with your spending habits.

» Gather required documents: You will need to provide personal information such as your Social Security number, income information, and employment status when you apply for a credit card. Make sure you have all the required documents handy.

» Apply online or in person: You can apply for a credit card online or at a bank or credit union. If you are under 21, you may need to show proof of income or have a co-signer on the account.

» Wait for approval: After submitting your application, the credit card issuer will review your application and credit history to determine whether to approve or deny your request. You will receive your card in the mail within a few weeks if approved.

CREDIT CARD VS. DEBIT CARD

There are two common ways to pay without using cash: credit cards and debit cards. What's the difference between them? You can learn everything you need to know right here.

Credit Cards

» Credit cards let you borrow money from the card company to buy stuff.
» You need to pay back what you borrow, usually with extra money called interest.
» The card company sets a limit on how much you can borrow.
» If you use your credit card responsibly, it can help you build your credit history.
» Some credit cards give you rewards, like cash back or points, when you use them.
» Some credit cards charge you money every year just for having them.
» Credit cards have policies to protect you from fraud.

Debit Cards

» Debit cards let you spend money you already have in your bank account.
» You don't have to pay back any money you spend with your debit card.
» There's no limit on how much you can spend, but you can only spend what's in your account.
» Using your debit card doesn't help you build credit history.
» Debit cards usually don't give you rewards for using them.
» Most debit cards don't have annual fees.
» Debit cards also have policies to protect you from fraud.

BUILDING CREDIT

Building a good credit history in your teen years is not only possible but very, very important! When you have an excellent credit history behind you, things will be a lot easier for you later on.

HOW IS CREDIT SCORE CALCULATED?

Basically, credit scoring models look at a few different things:

- » Your payment history
- » The amount of debt you have
- » The length of your credit history
- » Any new credit you've recently applied for.

They use this information to give you a number between 300 and 850, your credit score.

For example, let's say you just got a credit card, and you've been using it responsibly, paying your bill on time and in full every month. This will likely help boost your credit score since it shows you can handle credit responsibly.

On the other hand, if you've missed a few payments or maxed out your credit card, your credit score could take a hit. That's why it's essential to be mindful of your credit usage and pay your bills on time to keep your score in good shape.

BEGIN TODAY:
FIRST STEPS TO ESTABLISHING A GOOD CREDIT HISTORY.

Building a credit history is essential because it can affect your loan, credit card, and even apartment approval. Credit histories show how you've handled credit in the past, and lenders and other financial institutions use them to determine your creditworthiness. It can also help you get better interest rates, loan terms, and even a better job. However, it can be tricky to know where to start. Here's how to build a credit history:

- » Get a credit card: The first step is getting a credit card. You may need to start with a secured credit card, which requires a deposit, or a student credit card with a lower credit limit. Use the credit card for small purchases, and make sure to pay off the balance in full every month to avoid interest charges.
- » Pay your bills on time: Paying your bills, such as your phone bill, on time is vital for establishing a good credit history. Late payments can negatively impact your credit score, which is a number that represents your creditworthiness.
- » Check your credit report: Your credit report records your credit history, including

95

loans, credit cards, and payment history. You can request a free copy of your credit report once a year from each of the three major credit bureaus: Equifax, Experian, and TransUnion. Don't forget to check your credit report for errors.

» Become an authorized user: If you have a family member or friend with a good credit history, you can ask them to add you to their credit card account. This can help you build a credit history, but be aware that any missed payments or high balances can negatively impact both your credit scores.

» Be patient: Building a good credit history takes time. It's essential to be patient and responsible with your credit usage. Avoid opening too many credit accounts simultaneously, as this can negatively impact your credit score.

By following these tips, you can start building a solid credit history that will serve you well in the future. Remember to use your credit responsibly and pay your bills on time to maintain your credit score.

Did you know you can check your credit report for free once a year? It's true! Head to *AnnualCreditReport.com* to get a copy of your report from each of the three credit bureaus. It's crucial to check your report regularly to make sure everything is accurate and to catch any errors or fraud.

Now that you understand credit scores better let's flip the coin and focus on the other side: debt.

WHAT THE HECK IS DEBT?

It's essential to understand what debt is to make informed decisions about managing your money. Debt is simply money you owe to someone else. There are many types of debt, such as credit card debt, student loan debt, and medical debt. Understanding the different types of debt is the first step in taking control of your finances.

> Debt is simply money you owe to someone else.

DIFFERENT TYPES OF DEBT
(CREDIT CARD DEBT, STUDENT LOAN DEBT, ETC.)

As you navigate the world of personal finance, it's essential to understand the different types of debt and how they can impact your financial well-being. Let's dive into the various categories of debt.

» Secured Debt: This type of debt is backed by an asset, such as a home or car. Simply put, you borrow money and give the lender something as collateral. If you can't repay the loan, they can take what you bought away from you. For example, when you buy a car with a loan, the car itself is the collateral. If you stop making payments, the lender can take the car back.

» Unsecured Debt: This type of debt is not backed by an asset but by your creditworthiness. If you default on the loan, they might take legal action but can't take away your stuff. For example, credit card debt is unsecured debt.

» Revolving Debt: You can borrow money up to a specific limit, pay it off, and borrow more as needed. Credit cards are the most common example of revolving debt.

» Installment Debt: This type of debt has a set repayment schedule, with a fixed amount due each month until the loan is paid in full. Mortgages and auto loans are examples of installment debt.

Understanding the different types of debt and their terms and conditions is crucial for making informed decisions about borrowing and managing your money. It's essential to carefully consider the terms of any loan, including interest rates, fees, and repayment schedules, and to borrow only what you can afford to repay. By staying informed and making responsible choices, you can avoid debt traps and build a solid financial future.

IS DEBT GOING TO AFFECT MY FINANCES?

It's easy to get caught up in the excitement of buying things you want, but it's essential to consider the long-term impact on your finances. If you make the minimum payments, you will be faced with high-interest debt. While it might be tempting, you should understand that it will negatively impact your finances.

When you have high-interest debt, like credit card debt or payday loans, you end up paying more in interest over time. For example, let's say you buy a new gaming system for $500 on your credit card with a 20% interest rate. Suppose you only make the minimum monthly payment. In that case, it could take you over 3 years to pay off the balance, and you'll end up paying over $300 in interest alone! That's like buying another gaming system just in interest!

High-interest debt costs you more money and makes it harder to save for things important to you, like college or a car. When you're stuck making minimum payments on your debt, you're not progressing toward your financial goals.

So, before swiping that credit card, consider the long-term impact on your finances. Remember, living within your means and avoiding the debt web is essential!

I'M ALREADY IN DEBT: WHAT CAN I DO?

It's hard to manage debt, but with some planning and effort, you can regain control. Here are some tips to help you get started.

» Start by creating a debt repayment plan.

The first step to managing your debt is to create a repayment plan. This involves taking stock of all your debts, including the amount owed, interest rates, and payment due dates. Once you have this information, you can create a plan prioritizing which debts to pay off first. For example, you may want to focus on paying off high-interest debts first, like credit card debt, before tackling lower-interest debts, like student loans.

» Choose the strategy you'll use for paying off debt

You can pay off your debt using several strategies, including:

Debt Snowball: This strategy involves paying off your smallest debts first while making minimum payments on larger debts. Once you pay off a smaller debt, you can use the extra money to pay off larger debts, which can help you build momentum and stay motivated.

Debt Avalanche: This strategy involves paying off your debts in order of highest to lowest interest rates. By tackling high-interest debts first, you can save on interest charges and pay off your debts faster.

Balance Transfer: Basically, this strategy consists of moving your high-interest credit card debt to a new credit card with a lower interest rate. You can save money on interest charges and pay off your debt faster, but remember to read the fine print and watch out for balance transfer fees.

Remember, managing debt takes time and effort, but with a solid plan and a little discipline, you can take control of your finances and achieve your financial goals.

WHAT IF I DEFAULT ON MY DEBT?

Defaulting your debt can have serious consequences. It can damage your credit score, making it difficult to get approved for loans or credit cards in the future. Suppose you default on a student loan, for example. In that case, the government can garnish your wages or even take your tax refund to collect the debt.

In some cases, defaulting on debt can even lead to legal action, such as wage garnishment or a lawsuit. It's essential always to make your payments on time and work with your creditors if you're having trouble making payments.

Managing credit and debt can be a challenging task. Still, taking responsibility for your financial decisions is essential to avoid getting into debt. While buying things beyond your means can be tempting, avoiding debt is the wisest thing to do. This does not mean you should never get into debt, but you need to be smart about it. Here are some tips for responsible borrowing:

- » Only borrow what you can afford to pay back
- » Shop around for the best interest rates and terms
- » Read the fine print and understand the terms and conditions of any loan or credit agreement
- » If you already have debt on your back, focus on creating a debt repayment plan and stick to it
- » Build an emergency fund to avoid using credit cards for unexpected expenses

It's easy to get caught up in wanting things beyond our means, just like the little mermaid who took on debt to achieve her dreams. However, the little mermaid learned that happiness comes from being true to yourself and making responsible choices. In the same way, make sure you prioritize your financial well-being and make responsible choices when it comes to credit and debt. A solid financial future starts with living within your means, carefully budgeting, and borrowing responsibly.

Activity 1: Debit or Credit?

Take a look at the information in the first column. Decide whether a debit card or a credit card was used and put an X in the correct column.

TRANSACTION	DEBIT CARD	CREDIT CARD
Tom goes to the bank machine and withdraws $100 from his bank account using her card.	☐	☐
Your uncle takes you out for lunch and pays with a card. The money comes out of her bank account.	☐	☐
Your mom takes you to get your nails done. She pays with a card and tells you she'll pay for it at the end of the month when she gets her bill.	☐	☐
Your sister takes you shopping for back to school clothes. She pays with a card and asks to do it in three installments.	☐	☐
You go to the doctor and your dad pays with a card. The payment comes out of his bank account.	☐	☐
You and your family are going to Disneyland. Your dad buys the tickets to the parks with a card. The money comes out of his bank account.	☐	☐
Jane received a monthly bill for her card. She has used the card a lot this month and is unable to pay off the total bill. She is very unhappy because she is going to have to pay interest.	☐	☐
Your mom goes grocery shopping with a card. The bill shows up on her monthly card statement. She can pay the bill in full and does not have to pay interest.	☐	☐

*Reach out to aempub@gmail.com for your free answer sheet!

Activity 2: "Mastering Debt

A STEP-BY-STEP REPAYMENT PLAN"

Emily has multiple debts, can you help her organize her payment plan? Create a plan for paying off the debts according to the strategy you chose.

Emily

Meet Emily, a 22-year-old college graduate who has accumulated multiple debts while in school. She has the following debts:

» Student Loan: $10,000 at 5% interest rate
» Credit Card 1: $2,000 at 18% interest rate
» Credit Card 2: $4,500 at 22% interest rate
» Personal Loan: $3,500 at 12% interest rate

Emily works full-time and has a monthly income of $3,000. She currently pays the minimum amount due on each of her debts, but she wants to create a plan to pay them off faster and save money on interest charges.

1. After reading through the chapter about credit and debt, choose one of the debt repayment strategies discussed in the chapter: Debt Snowball, Debt Avalanche, or Balance Transfer.
2. Read the information about Emily's debt and write down the name of each debt, the amount owed, and the interest rate.

DEBT	AMOUNT	INTEREST RATE

3. Using the debt repayment strategy you chose, decide the steps you'll follow to pay off each debt.

DEBT REPAYMENT STRATEGY: _____

4. For each debt, calculate how much you will pay each month and how long it will take to pay it off.

5. Reflect on your plan and think about how you can incorporate responsible borrowing habits into your financial decisions in the future.

EXAMPLE: DEBT SNOWBALL STRATEGY

» Step 1: Make a list of all the debts in order from smallest balance to largest balance.

- Credit Card 1:
  $2,000 at 18% interest rate
- Personal Loan:
  $3,500 at 12% interest rate
- Credit Card 2:
  $4,500 at 22% interest rate
- Student Loan:
  $10,000 at 5% interest rate

» Step 2: Continue making minimum payments on all debts except the smallest one (Credit Card 1). Use any extra money in your budget to pay off this debt as quickly as possible. Once it's paid off, move to the next smallest debt (Personal Loan) and repeat the process.

- Credit Card 1:
  $2,000 at 18% interest rate (pay $200 per month)
- Personal Loan:
  $3,500 at 12% interest rate (pay $350 per month)
- Credit Card 2:
  $4,500 at 22% interest rate (pay minimum payment of $112 per month)
- Student Loan:
  $10,000 at 5% interest rate (pay minimum payment of $150 per month)

» Step 3: As you pay off each debt, roll over the money you were using to make payments on the previous debt to the next one. This will create a "snowball effect" and help you pay off larger debts faster.

- Credit Card 1:
  Paid off in 10 months
- Personal Loan:
  $3,500 at 12% interest rate (pay $550 per month)
- Credit Card 2:
  $4,500 at 22% interest rate (pay $662 per month)
- Student Loan:
  $10,000 at 5% interest rate (pay $812 per month)

CHAPTER 6

Key takeaways

» Credit allows you to buy things you couldn't afford otherwise. By using credit responsibly, you can build your credit history and make qualifying for loans and credit cards easier. There are three main types of credit, investment credit, commercial credit and consumer credit

» The common ways to pay without using cash are credit cards and debit cards. Debit cards let you spend money you already have in your bank account. Credit cards let you borrow money from the card company to buy stuff.

» Types of credit cards: major department stores, bank cards and travel and entertainment cards. When you use a credit card to make a purchase, you'll get a bill in the mail within a month. Depending on the type of credit card you've used, the store will get paid differently.

» Getting a credit card is not as difficult as you might think, you need to check the age requirement, research, gather the required documents, apply online or in person and wait for approval:

» Building a good credit history in your teen years is not only possible but very, very important

» Debt is simply money you owe to someone else. There are many types of debt, such as credit card debt, student loan debt, and medical debt. Secured Debt, unsecured Debt, revolving Debt, installment Debt:

» It's essential to carefully consider the terms of any loan, including interest rates, fees, and repayment schedules, and to borrow only what you can afford to repay, so you can consider the long-term impact on your finances. When you have high-interest debt, like credit card debt or payday loans, you end up paying more in interest over time

» When having a debt you can start by creating a debt repayment plan and choose from the types of strategy one you'll use for paying off debt

Chapter 7

Giving Back

"No one has ever become poor by giving."
Anne Frank.

AS A TEENAGER, YOU MAY FEEL LIKE YOU NEED TO BE A SUPERHERO OR A MILLIONAIRE TO MAKE A DIFFERENCE IN THE WORLD. BUT THAT'S FAR FROM THE TRUTH!

Giving a little bit of what you have to the people around you can have a significant impact on their lives. Shuri, Blank Panther's sister, is a great example of this. Shuri is responsible for developing the advanced technology of Wakanda, using it to help her brother and the rest of the Wakandan people. The movie shows a generous girl who is kind to those around her. We can all strive to be like that without the need to be in a Marvel movie.

Understanding how to give back to the community is crucial. We have already seen how to make and save money. Our community service shows that we're thankful for what we have and understand that others have different opportunities and resources. Giving back helps us cultivate compassion, empathy, and kindness.

This chapter will explore the importance of giving back and, most importantly, how to do it. There are thousands of ways you can make a difference, and we'll give you some ideas on how to get started.

Remember, you don't need to be a superhero to make a difference. All you need is a kind heart and a willingness to help others. So let's dive right in and explore the world of giving back!

GIVING BACK

How often do you hear the phrase "giving back"? It means helping someone without expecting anything in return. And let me tell you, giving back is super important! Booker T. Washington once said that those who do the most for others are the happiest.

It is possible to help others in many different ways. You could volunteer at a local charity or non-profit organization or donate some of your time and energy to help out a neighbor or friend. It can also mean donating money or goods to a charity or cause you care about.

By doing this, you can make a difference and feel good about yourself. You never know what impact you could have when you give back!

GIVING BACK: WHY IS IT IMPORTANT?

First of all, let's talk about how giving back helps others. You can positively impact someone's life when you do something nice or helpful for them. Whether volunteering at a local soup kitchen, donating clothes to a homeless shelter, or simply helping a neighbor carry groceries, these small acts of kindness can go a long way in making someone else's day a little brighter.

Additionally, giving back can positively impact our communities. When you unite with those around you to support causes and organizations you care about, you can create real change and make a difference.

THE BENEFITS OF GIVING BACK.

As the old saying goes, it feels good to do good. Unexpectedly, giving back comes with many benefits, making us more inclined to continue doing so. Among the benefits are the following:

 It feels good: Helping others can give you a sense of fulfillment and happiness. Stress can also be reduced, and your mood can be boosted.

It enhances personal growth: Giving back can help you learn new skills, like empathy, compassion, and teamwork, and gain new experiences. You'll get a better understanding of people's struggles and challenges, so you can relate to them better. In addition, doing something kind or generous for someone else boosts your self-esteem and makes you feel good about yourself.

It can make a difference: Giving back can have a real impact on the lives of others, whether it's through donating to a charity or volunteering your time. Knowing that you're making a difference can be incredibly rewarding.

WAYS TO GIVE BACK TO THE COMMUNITY

It's common to feel like your efforts won't make a difference in today's world. But that's not true! No matter how small your actions are, you can never know the impact they will have. There are thousands of ways to give back without spending much time or money.

One way to give back is through volunteering. This can involve anything like baking cookies for your local firefighters to tutoring students after school. Each and every bit counts!

Another way to give back is by donating. You can donate money to a charity or cause you care about or donate goods like clothes, food, or toys.

There's also fundraising. This involves raising money for a charity or causes through events like bake sales, car washes, or charity runs. Fundraising can be a lot of fun, and it's a great way to bring people together for a good cause.

The important thing is to choose the method of giving back that feels comfortable and fulfilling for you. Each type of contribution has unique characteristics, so learning about them and choosing the path that speaks to you is essential. Take a closer look at the different ways you can give.

Volunteering

You've heard of volunteering, right? Volunteering is the act of giving your time and energy to help others without receiving any financial compensation.[1] You can volunteer in many ways, from helping out at a local non-profit organization to participating in community service projects. The opportunities are endless, and volunteering can be a gratifying experience.

BENEFITS OF VOLUNTEERING

Here are just a few of the trillions of benefits volunteerism has to offer:

1. When volunteering, you get directly involved with the people and organizations you are helping. You get to see firsthand the impact your time and effort have on the community. Whether helping at a local food bank or participating in a community cleanup, you are physically there, making a difference.
2. Volunteering can also give you a sense of purpose and fulfillment. Knowing that you contribute to something larger than yourself can be incredibly rewarding.
3. It can allow you to meet new people and expand your social network. You can connect with like-minded individuals who share your passion for helping others. This can be especially beneficial for teenagers like yourself, who want to make new friends or find a sense of belonging.

DIFFERENT TYPES OF VOLUNTEERING OPPORTUNITIES[2]

Volunteering comes in many forms, so when choosing, consider all your options:

ANIMAL VOLUNTEER WORK

Volunteering with animals is a great way to give back to the community while helping our furry friends. A plus: getting to spend time with some cute animals. You can help at a local animal shelter by cleaning cages, feeding animals, and walking dogs. If you have a passion for wildlife, you can also go a little further and volunteer at a wildlife rehabilitation center. For example, you could count penguins on Phillip Island, protect turtle eggs from predators in Costa Rica, or support community efforts to rehabilitate elephants in Asia.

SOCIAL VOLUNTEER WORK

This is about supporting and helping people in your community who need help. It can involve various activities, such as mentoring kids or providing food and shelter for people without homes.

Getting involved with social causes can make a huge difference in someone's life, and it's also a great way to meet new people and expand your social circle. These are some ideas:

» Teaching: become a volunteer teacher at home and abroad for people in need.
» Working with children and youth: Volunteering with youth clubs, schools, scouts, or summer camps are a popular type of volunteering work for high school students who are active and outgoing.

HEALTHCARE VOLUNTEER WORK

Healthcare volunteer work can literally change people's lives. There are many ways to get involved, whether it's helping out at a local hospital, nursing home, or clinic. As a healthcare volunteer, you might help with tasks like greeting patients, answering phones, or delivering supplies. You might also work directly with patients, like reading to children in a hospital or providing companionship to elderly residents in a nursing home. It can be a very rewarding experience as you get to help others in need and learn about the healthcare industry. If you don't know were to start, you can try working with geriatrics as a volunteer. The area offers many opportunities, from delivering Meals on Wheels to helping an elderly grocery shopper or simply calling each morning and checking in.

ENVIRONMENTAL VOLUNTEER WORK

If you care about the planet and want to make a difference, environmental work might be for you. This could include participating in beach cleanups, planting trees, or working on conservation projects in national parks. Not only will you be contributing to important efforts to protect the environment, but you'll also be able to meet like-minded people who share your passion for sustainability.

Plus, spending time outside and connecting with nature can be fulfilling and rewarding. Some ideas are:

» Tasks such as reforestation, cleaning up beaches, nature trail construction, and invasive species management.

» Joining a climate change volunteer project. This may be by volunteering with environmental groups, or forming a local political group to help to create genuine political change.

HOW TO FIND VOLUNTEERING OPPORTUNITIES IN YOUR COMMUNITY

The first step is to get moving! Don't wait for opportunities to come to you - actively seek them out. Use your network of family and friends. Ask if anyone knows of any local organizations or events that need volunteers. You might be surprised by how much information you can gather by reaching out to the people in your life.

Another option is to use websites like VolunteerMatch, which can connect you with various volunteer opportunities in your area. Simply create a profile and search for opportunities based on your interests, skills, and availability. You can even set up alerts to receive notifications when new opportunities become available.

Donating

Donating is all about selflessness. It is the act of giving money, goods, or services to someone or an organization in need, usually to a non-profit or charity organization.[3] Donations come in various forms, from one-time gifts to recurring, regular contributions. No matter how big or small, every donation counts and can make a significant difference in someone's life.

THE IMPORTANCE OF DONATING TO A CAUSE.

Donating to a cause is a great way to support something you care about, whether it's a charity, a non-profit organization, or a specific cause or campaign. Sometimes it's impossible to volunteer your time. However, you can still make a positive impact by donating money to support a cause that you are passionate about.

If you donate money, you can help fund research for a disease, provide food and shelter for those in need, or support an animal welfare organization. Consider supporting a cause or organization that aligns with your values. You can research online to find reputable organizations or even ask for recommendations from friends and family.

HOW TO CHOOSE A CHARITY TO DONATE TO

When it comes to choosing a charity to donate to, it's important to find a cause that you feel passionate about. This could be anything from protecting the environment to supporting education or fighting poverty. Take some time to think about what matters most to you and what you want to support, you can write your ideas here!

Once you know the cause you wish to donate to, search for organizations aligning with your values. Make sure to read up on their mission and values to ensure they are aligned with your own beliefs. You want to make sure that your donation will be put to good use and will impact the cause you care about.

DIFFERENT WAYS TO DONATE.

Depending on your preferences, resources, and cause, donations can be made in a variety of ways:

 Monetary donations: The most common way to donate is to give money to a charity or non-profit organization. You can donate online, by mail, or in person. Some charities also accept donations via text message or social media.

 Donating goods: You can also donate physical goods, such as clothing, food, furniture, or toys. Some charities have specific needs for certain goods, so it's a good idea to check with the organization first.

 Donating blood or plasma: Blood and plasma donations are always in high demand, especially during times of crisis or emergency. You can donate at a local blood bank or donation center.

There are many ways to donate, so keep looking if none of these appeal to you. The options are endless!

STARTING A CHARITABLE PROJECT

Would you like to contribute to your community in an original way? Starting a charitable project might be how to do so!

To create a successful charitable project, it's essential to be aware of the realities of your community and the specific needs that should be addressed. With creativity and effort, you can bring about positive change in the world and make a difference. Here's how to do it in simple steps.

IDENTIFYING A NEED IN THE COMMUNITY

The first step to creating a charitable project is identifying a need in the community and brainstorming ideas for a project that will address that need.

Your community's needs

The process of brainstorming ideas may involve researching successful projects in other communities, speaking with community members who have dealt with similar issues, or simply using your creativity.

A Guide to Brainstorming

TOPIC: _____

INSTRUCTIONS:

» Write down as many ideas as you can think of related to the topic.

» Don't judge or criticize any ideas, no matter how wild or unconventional they may seem.

» Try to come up with as many ideas as possible within the time limit provided.

Write your ideas here:

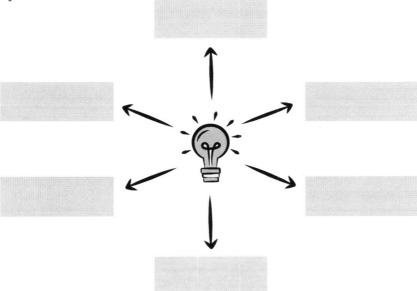

REFLECTION:

Which ideas do you think are the strongest?

Are there any ideas that you think could be combined or expanded upon?

What insights or perspectives did you gain from this brainstorming exercise?

How might you apply these insights to your life or future projects?

Remember, brainstorming is just one tool for generating ideas. Keep an open mind and continue to explore different approaches and perspectives as you work on your projects. Good luck!

PLANNING A CHARITABLE PROJECT

It's important to keep in mind that starting a charitable project can be a challenging and time-consuming process, but it can also be incredibly rewarding.

To successfully launch and run a charitable project, it's essential to have a solid plan in place. This should include identifying goals and objectives, creating a budget, establishing a timeline, and assembling a team of volunteers to help you bring your project to life.

RECRUITING VOLUNTEERS FOR THE PROJECT.

Recruiting volunteers is crucial to the success of your charitable project. It can be done in several ways. Get the word out about your project by using social media. Invite your friends and family to share your project on their Facebook, Twitter, and Instagram pages.

Another way to recruit volunteers is to promote your project to people you know. Tell your friends, family, and acquaintances about the project and ask if they would be interested in helping.

Creating a space for volunteers to connect and feel like they are part of something bigger is also important. This could be a Facebook group or a chat group where volunteers can communicate with each other, share ideas, and ask for help when needed. Encouraging volunteers to bond can help create a sense of community and motivation to keep working toward the project's goals.

FUNDRAISING

Fundraising is a way of collecting money or resources for a good cause. It involves a range of activities, from organizing events to selling products or seeking donations from individuals or organizations.

DIFFERENT TYPES OF FUNDRAISING EVENTS[4]

1. Fun-run walk: You could organize a hiking trail and charge participants an entry fee. This does not include marathons, half-marathons, 5Ks, or other high-profile races. Fun runs, and walks are the most accessible fundraising campaign events to plan and deliver a high return on investment for organizations of all sizes.

2. Competition (non-sport): If you're not into sports, don't worry! You can still organize a competition as a fundraiser. For example, you could hold a trivia night, a baking competition, or a video game tournament. Charge people to enter the competition and offer prizes to the winners.

3. Fashion show: Show off new styles in a fashion show fundraiser that gets everyone involved. You could get local designers or boutiques to donate clothes and charge people to attend the show. You could also sell the clothes after the show to raise even more money.

4. Auction: An auction fundraising event gives your guests a reason to open their wallets and something to do while socializing. It is a great way to raise money if you have some valuable items to sell.

5. Concert: Benefit concerts aren't just the celebrity performer-packed events you see on television. Concerts can also be smaller scale, featuring local talent.

PLANNING A FUNDRAISING EVENT.

You need to consider a few things when organizing a fundraising event:

1. Select a type of fundraising you feel more inclined to do: Are you thinking of a bake sale, a car wash, or maybe even a talent show? Whatever you choose, make sure it's something you're excited about, as that will help motivate you to put in the work needed to make it a success.

2. Seek out a place to do it: Once you've got the type of event nailed down, it's time to start looking for a location. This will depend on the event you're organizing.

3. Invite people: Reach out to your friends, family, and anyone else you think would be interested in attending your event. You can make flyers and post them around town, create a social media event, or even send out personal invitations.

4. Plan how the day will be: Make sure you have all the necessary supplies and equipment for your event. Plan out the day's schedule, leaving plenty of time for set-up and tear-down.

5. Enjoy: it's time to enjoy the event you've organized! Make sure you plan some fun activities or games to keep your attendees engaged and entertained.

RECRUITING VOLUNTEERS FOR THE EVENT

Now that you've got your fundraising event planned, it's time to recruit some volunteers to help you succeed! The first step in recruiting volunteers is to create a post on social media. This could be on Instagram, Facebook, Twitter, or any other social media platform that you and your friends use.

When recruiting volunteers, you must be clear about what you're expecting from them. Provide clear instructions and guidelines, and be upfront about any required training or qualifications. This will help ensure that your volunteers are prepared and ready to help when the day of the event arrives.

Once you've posted your call for volunteers on social media, be prepared to follow up with interested individuals.

MEASURING THE IMPACT

Whether you're creating your own charitable project or organizing a fundraising event, it's always important to measure impact! Humans are naturally curious about how their actions and efforts affect the world around them.

Understanding the impact of your work is vital for growth and improvement. In this context, measuring the impact of your charitable project allows you to assess the consequences and outcomes of your actions and determine whether they align with your goals and objectives.

WAYS TO MEASURE THE IMPACT OF A CHARITABLE PROJECT

Start by asking the people directly impacted by your project for their feedback. Their evaluation can help you understand how your work has affected them and if there are any areas for improvement. It's essential to listen to and consider their opinions when planning future projects.

Another way to measure impact is by taking the time to make a self-evaluation yourself. Think about what you set out to achieve and whether you accomplished it. Consider how you can improve the project in the future and what new goals you can set.

Taking before and after pictures of the work done is also a great way to gain visibility of the change you've made. This not only helps you measure the project's impact but also creates a visual representation of the work you've done.

THE IMPORTANCE OF EVALUATING A PROJECT'S IMPACT

First up, it can inspire others. When people see your project's impact, it can motivate them to get involved and make a difference too. It's like a ripple effect - one small project can greatly impact a larger community.

Another positive aspect of evaluating impact is that if you're working on a project involving any funding or sponsorship, evaluating your impact can be crucial. Sponsors want to know that their money is going toward something that's making a real difference. By showing them the impact your project is having, you can help secure more funding for future projects.

COLLABORATION WITH OTHER ORGANIZATIONS

Now that you know how to do a charity project, you need to figure out how bigger organizations can help. Asking for help can be intimidating. Still, if you ask for support from organizations, you can give back more than you would by working independently.

That's where the 3 C's come in - Choose, Contact, and Collaborate. It's a simple principle that can help you navigate this process.

» Choose: think about what kind of organizations or groups you might want to collaborate with. Maybe there's a local non-profit that's working on a similar issue or a community group that has resources that could help your project.

» Contact: Once you've chosen a few potential collaborators, it's time to contact them. This can be as simple as sending an email or making a phone call to introduce yourself and your project. Don't worry too much about sounding professional or formal - just be yourself and explain what you're working on and why you think collaboration could be beneficial.

» Collaborate: This is where you'll work together to figure out how you can support each other's goals and make a bigger impact in the community. It might mean sharing resources, coordinating events, or even combining projects to make them more effective.

THE BENEFIT OF COLLABORATION

Collaboration is an essential element of success in any field. Working with others can bring numerous benefits to help you achieve your goals faster and more efficiently. Here are some benefits collaborations bring:

1. Monetary: By pooling resources and sharing expenses, you can reduce the costs associated with any project
2. Visibility: Working with others means tapping into their network, expanding your reach and exposure to potential clients, investors, and partners
3. Get work off your shoulders: Working on a project alone can be overwhelming and time-consuming, leading to burnout and decreased productivity. By collaborating with others, you can share the workload, delegate tasks, and focus on your strengths.

INSPIRING OTHERS

It was said by Ken Poirot that "Greatness comes from inspiring others to be their best". It is not just you who can make a difference when working. You and those you inspire are the ones who can make the biggest difference.

HOW TO INSPIRE OTHERS TO GIVE BACK TO THE COMMUNITY

As a leader, you should learn how to inspire others so they want to give back as much as you want.

You have to show them what it feels like to give back. It is sometimes true that people don't contribute to others because they have never experienced the feeling of working toward others. Show them how nice it feels with your own testimony.

PLANNING FOR LONG-TERM GIVING

Taking care of others doesn't have to be something you do sporadically; it can be part of your daily life. Hence, planning for long-term giving is essential.

HOW TO MAKE GIVING BACK A LONG-TERM HABIT

Giving back a long-term habit requires commitment, consistency, and finding a cause that aligns with your values and interests. Here are some tips on how to make giving back a regular part of your life:

1. Set a goal: Decide how often you want to give back and how much time or money you want to donate. Start small and gradually increase your commitment over time.

2. Find a cause you're passionate about: Identify a cause that resonates with you, whether it's environmental conservation, social justice, education, or animal welfare. Research organizations in that area and find one that aligns with your values.

3. Schedule giving back activities: Make giving back a regular part of your schedule. Schedule volunteer activities, donation drives, or fundraising events regularly, such as once a month or once a quarter.

4. Share with others: Talk to friends and family about your commitment to giving back. Share stories about the impact of your contributions and invite others to join you in your efforts.

5. Track your progress: Keep a record of your giving back activities and track your progress over time. Celebrate your achievements and use them as motivation to continue your efforts.

6. Get involved with a community: Join a community of like-minded individuals who share your commitment to giving back. This can give you support, encouragement, and inspiration to continue your efforts.

Remember that giving back is a journey, not a destination. It takes time and effort to establish a regular habit, but the rewards of making a positive impact in the world are immeasurable.

1   Merriam-Webster. (n.d.). Volunteer Definition & meaning. Merriam-Webster. Retrieved March 28, 2023, from https://www.merriam-webster.com/dictionary/volunteer

2   Turnbull, A. (2021, September 2). 12 different types of volunteering work you can try. Rosterfy. Retrieved March 28, 2023, from https://www.rosterfy.com/blog/12-different-types-of-volunteering-work-you-can-try-rosterfy.

3   Merriam-Webster. (n.d.). Donate definition & meaning. Merriam-Webster. Retrieved March 31, 2023, from https://www.merriam-webster.com/dictionary/donate#: :text=transitive%20verb,a%20public%20or%20charitable%20cause

4   Which type of fundraising event is best for your nonprofit? Classy. (2023, March 15). Retrieved March 29, 2023, from https://www.classy.org/blog/which-type-of-fundraising-event-is-best-for-your-nonprofit/

LET'S WORK TOGETHER

TASK: CREATE YOUR OWN FUNDRAISING PROJECT!

» Your reasons for wanting to raise money

» What type of fundraising do you want to do?

» What do you need for this fundraising? (Write all elements needed)

» Place your are doing this

» Write the people you want to invite

» Make a schedule of your fundraising day

CHAPTER 7

Key takeaways

» Giving back means helping someone without expecting anything. It is possible to give back in many different ways. Maybe you volunteer at a local charity or donate something. You can positively impact someone's life when you do something friendly or helpful for them. Benefits of giving back: it feels good, it enhances personal growth, it can make a difference:

» Volunteering: Volunteering is the act of getting directly involved with the people and organizations that give you a sense of purpose and fulfillment. There is animal volunteer work, social volunteer work, healthcare volunteer work, and environmental volunteer work.

» Donating is giving money, goods, or services to someone or an organization in need, usually to a non-profit or charity organization. Finding a cause, you feel passionate about donating to is essential. There are monetary donations, donating goods, or donating blood or plasma.

» A successful charitable project starts with being aware of the realities of your community and the specific needs that should be addressed. Recruiting volunteers is crucial to the success of your charitable project. It can be done in several ways.

» Fundraising involves various activities, from organizing events to selling products or seeking donations from individuals or organizations. There are different types: fun-run walk, competition (non-sport), fashion show and others.

» By evaluating the impact of your charitable project, you can determine whether your goals and objectives are aligned with the results. You can ask the people who have been directly impacted by your project for their feedback or by taking the time to make a self-evaluation yourself.

» There are several benefits that come with collaboration, monetary, visibility , and get work off your shoulders

» Planning for long-term giving is essential. You should set a goal, find a cause you're passionate about, and schedule giving-back activities

Chapter 8

College
and Career
Planning

"The future belongs to those who believe
in the beauty of their dreams."
Eleanor Roosevelt

You've probably taken plenty of road trips with your family. Planning and saving up for a successful trip is super important, right? Well, the same goes for your future college and career goals. It might not be the most exciting thing to think about right now, but trust me, it's worth it in the long run.

I know it can feel weird and exhausting to think about your future when you're young and just want to live in the moment. But taking the time to plan and prepare financially will make your journey a lot smoother. A great way to handle this situation is to know what to expect and be prepared to handle any costs.

I'm sure you've heard about loans and debt that comes with going to college. It's true, some people spend years paying off their college debt! But if you make a smart plan ahead of time, you might not have to deal with that burden for so long. That's why it's so important to start thinking about this stuff now, before it becomes a major stressor.

But don't worry, just because we're talking about the future doesn't mean you have to start freaking out. We're starting early so you can think clearly and calmly about everything, and make sure you're on the right track. In this chapter, we're going to cover all kinds of things, from the costs of college to how to save up for it and so much more. So buckle up and get ready for the ride, because we're just getting started!

UNDERSTANDING COLLEGE COSTS

Let's talk about the elephant in the room: college costs. We all know they aren't cheap, from tuition fees to textbooks and everything in between. But there's no need to panic! Understanding what you're getting into can help you plan ahead and start saving up some cash.

OVERVIEW OF COLLEGE COSTS:
TUITION, ROOM AND BOARD, BOOKS, AND FEES

It's no secret that going to college can put a dent in your wallet, so it's important to know exactly what you're getting into.

When you're looking at colleges, you'll often see a number called the "total cost of attendance". This includes not only tuition and fees, but also other expenses like books, supplies, transportation, and even housing. It's important to keep all of these costs in mind when you're making your decision.

Tuition and fees can vary widely depending on the college and the program you choose. Private colleges tend to be more expensive than public ones, and certain programs, like engineering or medicine, may cost more than others. You'll also want to look into any other fees that might be required, like lab fees or activity fees.

Housing is another major expense to consider. Some colleges include room and board in their total cost of attendance, while others don't. You'll have a variety of options for where to live, from on-campus dorms to off-campus apartments. If you're thinking about living off-campus, you'll also need to add to the total expense utilities, groceries, and transportation.

And let's not forget about textbooks and school supplies. These can add up quickly, with some textbooks costing hundreds of dollars each semester. One way to save money is to buy used textbooks or rent them instead of buying new ones. You can also check online for digital versions or even borrow them from the library. Overall, the cost of college can be pretty daunting.

COMPARISON OF IN-STATE, OUT-OF-STATE, AND PRIVATE COLLEGE COSTS

To make your search and decision easier it's essential to understand how prices differ among the various types of colleagues, so when you choose one, you know the real deal. Here is a comparative chart of in-state, out-of-state, and private college costs based on data from the College Board's 2021 Trends in College Pricing report:[1]

COLLEGE TYPE	AVERAGE TUITION & FEES (PER YEAR)	AVERAGE ROOM & BOARD (PER YEAR)	TOTAL COST (PER YEAR)
In-State	$10,560	$11,620	$22,180
Out-of-State	$27,020	$11,620	$38,640
Private	$38,330	$13,380	$51,710

As you can see, in-state colleges tend to be the most affordable option, with an average total cost of $22,180 per year. Out-of-state colleges are significantly more expensive, with an average total cost of $38,640 per year. Private colleges are the most expensive, with an average total cost of $51,710 per year.

Actual costs can vary widely depending on the college and program you choose. Additionally, these costs do not take into account any financial aid or scholarships that you may be eligible for, which can significantly reduce the cost of attending college.

When you're considering colleges, it's important to look at the total cost of attendance and not just the sticker price. You'll also want to consider factors like the quality of the program, the location of the college, and the available financial aid and scholarship options. With careful planning and budgeting, you can make attending college a reality, regardless of the cost.

WHAT ABOUT FINANCIAL AID AND SCHOLARSHIPS?

Financial aid and scholarships are important for students like you who are thinking about going to college. I'll go into more detail later, but let's start with the basics.

 Financial aid is money that is given or lent to students in order to help pay for their education. This can include different types of aid such as grants, loans, and work-study programs.

Federal financial aid is money that is given to students by the government in order to help pay for their college tuition and fees. This type of aid includes:

» Grants, which do not have to be repaid.

» Loans, which do have to be repaid with interest.

Student loans can come from two sources: federal financial aid or private lenders. Federal loans generally have lower interest rates than private loans, making them a more affordable option for students who need to borrow money to pay for college.

1. Federal student loans are offered by the government and typically have lower interest rates and more flexible repayment options than private loans. There are two types of federal loans: subsidized and unsubsidized. Subsidized loans do not accumulate interest while you are in school, while unsubsidized loans accumulate interest from the moment they are released.

2. Private loans, on the other hand, come from banks or other private lenders. These loans typically have higher interest rates than federal loans and may not offer the same flexible repayment options. However, private loans may be a good option for students who have exhausted their federal loan options or who have good credit and can qualify for lower interest rates.

 Scholarships are a type of financial aid that is awarded to students based on their academic or other achievements, such as athletic ability, community service, or artistic talent. Unlike loans, scholarships do not have to be repaid, making them a great option for students who need help paying for college but don't want to take on debt.

There are different types of scholarships available, including those offered by colleges and universities, private organizations, and corporations. Some scholarships are based on merit, while others are based on financial need. It's important to do your research and apply for as many scholarships as possible in order to maximize your chances of receiving aid.

STUDENT LOANS BECOME STUDENT DEBTS

It's key to remember that getting student loans means taking on debt, and debt can have long-term consequences. High levels of student debt can impact your credit score, make it harder to qualify for loans or credit cards in the future, and even affect your ability to buy a house or start a business. Plus, student loan debt typically cannot be discharged in bankruptcy, meaning you will be responsible for paying it back no matter what.

That's why it's important to borrow only what you need and to be mindful of your repayment options.

SAVING FOR COLLEGE

In previous chapters, we talked about different ways to save money. Saving for college, however, requires a different level of planning and preparation. There is no doubt that college is a major investment. As a result, you need to start thinking about college savings as soon as possible. We'll explore the various options available for saving for college, including 529 plans, custodial accounts, and more.

COLLEGE SAVINGS ACCOUNTS[2]

When saving for college, it's important to start early and have a solid plan in place. There are several saving accounts that are going to help you with that:

529 plan

This plan gives you tax benefits when you use it to pay for qualified education expenses. 529 plans can be used for college tuition, K-12 tuition, apprenticeship programs, and even student loan repayments. It is important to say that the amount you save with a 529 plan will not affect your financial aid eligibility.

Coverdell Education Savings Accounts (ESAs)

This type of Saving Accounts are tax-advantaged investment accounts designed to help families save for qualified education expenses. These expenses can include primary, secondary, or postsecondary education, as well as certain apprenticeship programs.

They offer several advantages for those who want to save for education expenses, including tax-free withdrawals when funds are used for qualified expenses. Additionally, the investments held in a Coverdell ESA can grow tax-free, meaning you won't owe taxes on any earnings until you withdraw the money.

•••

However, there are some restrictions to be aware of when it comes to Coverdell ESAs. First, beneficiaries must be under the age of 18 when the account is established. Contributions are also limited to $2,000 per child per year. And while the account can be used for various educational expenses, it must be used by the time the beneficiary reaches age 30 to avoid penalties and taxes.

Roth IRA and mutual fund

These are accounts that may offer more flexibility in terms of how you can use your savings, but they may also have different tax implications compared to 529 plans and Coverdell ESAs.

If you need help deciding which savings plan is best for you and your family, you can always talk to a financial advisor.

SAVING FOR COLLEGE 101

Savings can be totally manageable if you plan and prioritize. We've gone over the general ideas when it comes to saving money, but it's important to note that saving for college should be seen under a different light than the rest of your savings.

With such a big goal, you'll need a structured plan to follow, along with a different savings account and budgeting strategy.

One approach is to get a clear idea of the total expenses you will be facing, such as tuition, room and board, textbooks, and other fees. This will give you a benchmark to work towards and help you estimate how much money you need to save.

After calculating how much money you need to save, determine how much you can contribute each month to the amount you need to prepare for. It can be helpful to break it down into smaller, manageable steps, such as saving a certain amount per week or per paycheck. Creating a budget can also help you identify areas where you can cut back on expenses and put more towards your college savings.

It's important to keep track of your progress by annotating everything, including your expenses, savings, and any contributions you make to your college savings accounts. This can help you stay motivated and track your progress towards your goal.

By implementing these strategies and staying committed to your savings plan, you can take control of your college expenses and set yourself up for success in the future.

PAYING FOR COLLEGE

Similarly to saving for college, paying for it also requires careful planning and budgeting. It's important to prioritize your expenses and make informed decisions about how to allocate your resources. With some effort and dedication, you can find a way to pay for college as quick as possible and achieve your educational goals without getting overwhelmed by debt.

WORK-STUDY PROGRAMS

Work-study programs are a form of assistance that allows students to work part-time jobs on campus or off-campus to earn money to help pay for college expenses. These programs are available to undergraduate and graduate students who demonstrate financial need, and they offer a way for students to earn money to pay for educational expenses without accruing debt.

Colleges and universities typically offer work-study jobs such as library assistants, research assistants, and campus tour guides. Typically, work-study jobs pay at least the federal minimum wage and have flexible hours to accommodate students' academic schedules.

Work-study programs are other options for paying for college in the United States. It's important for students and their families to research and understand the costs and benefits of each option and to make an informed decision based on their individual financial situation and educational goals.

REPAYMENT PLANS FOR STUDENT LOANS

Federal loans offer a range of repayment plans, including income-driven plans that adjust your monthly payment based on your income and family size. This means that if you're earning a lower salary, you may be able to pay less each month towards your loan repayment. This can be a lifesaver for those who are struggling to make ends meet while also paying off their loans.

In addition to income-driven repayment plans, there are other options available for managing student loan debt. For example, graduates may consider consolidating their loans, which combines multiple loans into a single loan with a fixed interest rate. This can simplify the repayment process and may also result in a lower monthly payment.

Another option is deferment or forbearance, which allows borrowers to temporarily pause their loan payments if they are experiencing financial hardship or going back to school. While this can provide temporary relief, it's important to keep in mind that interest may continue to accrue during this time, which can result in a larger overall balance.

Finally, graduates may also be eligible for loan forgiveness programs, such as Public Service Loan Forgiveness (PSLF), which forgives remaining loan balances after 10 years of qualifying employment in the public sector. There are also loan forgiveness programs available for teachers, healthcare workers, and other professions.

Private lenders may offer similar options, but it's important to read the fine print and understand the terms of your loan before signing on the dotted line.

Remember, paying back your student loans may take time, but it's important to stay on top of your payments and make sure you're meeting your obligations. By taking advantage of repayment plans, working part-time while you study and carefully managing your finances, you can successfully pay off your loans and move forward with your life.

CHOOSING A CAREER PATH

At this point, you might be wondering, why did I get into this mess? How worthwhile is it? Well, it depends. The effort you put into building your professional career will be less satisfying if you don't have a purpose that reflects your interests. This means that if you're gonna work for something, it better be something you truly enjoy. In order to be sure of this, it's important to choose a career path carefully.

There are many career options available to teenagers today, and it can be difficult to choose one. You may feel overwhelmed and unsure about what you want to do with your life, and that's okay. It's important to remember that choosing a career path is a process, not a one-time decision.

HOW TO CHOOSE A CAREER

One of the most important factors to consider is your personal interests. It's essential to think about what you enjoy doing, what activities you find engaging, and what your natural talents are. These can all guide you towards a career that will be fulfilling and enjoyable for you.

Another important factor to consider is your values. Think about what is important to you in life, such as making a positive impact on the world, having a work-life balance, or earning a high salary. These values can help guide you towards a career that aligns with your goals and aspirations.

Job outlook is another important factor to consider when choosing a career path. It's important to research and understand the job market and demand for the career you're considering. Some careers have a higher demand than others, and this can impact your ability to find a job in your field and your earning potential.

Choosing a career path can be a challenging decision, but it's important to take your time and consider all factors before making a final decision. Remember that your career path can evolve and change over time, and it's okay to explore different options before settling on a specific career.

PREPARING FOR A CAREER

As a teenager, it's important to start taking steps towards achieving your future career. This means preparing yourself with the necessary knowledge and skills to enter the field you want to pursue.

When it comes to preparing for a career, education and training are crucial factors to consider. Your chosen career path may require specific degrees, certifications, or specialized training. Taking the time to invest in education and training can lead to greater opportunities, increased earning potential, and a more fulfilling career.

Many careers require a certain level of education, whether it be a high school diploma, an associate's degree, a bachelor's degree, or beyond. It is important to research the educational requirements for your chosen career path so you can plan accordingly. This may include taking specific classes in high school, attending a vocational or technical school, or pursuing a college or university degree.

In addition to education, specialized training can also be valuable in preparing for a career. This may include internships, apprenticeships, on-the-job training, or industry-specific certifications. These opportunities can provide hands-on experience and practical skills that will set you apart from other job applicants.

Investing in education and training for your chosen career path can also lead to greater job security and a more stable future. As the job market continues to change and evolve, having a strong foundation of education and training can give you the flexibility to adapt and pursue new opportunities.

WORK EXPERIENCE, INTERNSHIPS, AND APPRENTICESHIPS EXPLAINED

Internships, apprenticeships, and other work experience opportunities can be great ways for teenagers to gain valuable skills and experiences that can help them in college and beyond.

» Internships are typically short-term work experiences that allow students to gain practical, hands-on experience in a particular field. They may be paid or unpaid, and can be completed during the summer or during the school year. Internships can provide students with valuable skills, connections, and experience that can help them stand out when applying for jobs or further education.

» Apprenticeships are another type of work experience that allows students to gain skills and experience in a particular field. Apprenticeships typically involve on-the-job training and classroom instruction, and they are often paid. Apprenticeships are available in a wide range of fields, from construction and manufacturing to healthcare and technology. They can be a great way for students to gain valuable skills and experience while also earning a salary.

Overall, internships, apprenticeships, and other work experience opportunities can be great ways for you to gain valuable skills and experiences that can help you in college and beyond. These experiences can help you build you resume, develop professional skills, and make connections in their chosen field.

In conclusion, managing the costs of college can be a daunting task for teenagers, but it's important to remember that it's also an investment in your future. By carefully considering your options for financing your education, pursuing scholarships and grants, and taking advantage of opportunities to gain work experience, you can set yourself up for success both during and after college.

So, whether you're a high school student just starting to think about your college plans, or a college student navigating the challenges of financing your education, keep your eye on the prize and remember that with hard work and determination, you can achieve your goals and build a bright future.

1   Trends in college pricing: Highlights. Trends in College Pricing Highlights - College Board Research. (n.d.). Retrieved March 30, 2023, from https://research.collegeboard.org/trends/college-pricing/highlights

2   6 college savings accounts and how they work: BestColleges. BestColleges.com. (2022, February 11). Retrieved March 30, 2023, from https://www.bestcolleges.com/blog/college-savings-accounts/

LET'S WORK TOGETHER

TASK 1:

Are you curious about how successful university students managed to keep their finances in check? Now you can find out! This profile worksheet will allow you to gather insights and learn from different people who've navigated the challenges of university costs. Grab your pencil and get ready to be inspired by the stories of those who have successfully managed university costs!

REALITY CHECK:
UNIVERSITY COSTS

Name _____ Age _____ Gender _____
Current occupation _____
Highest Level of Education Completed _____

» What was your major in college/university?

» How did you pay for tuition and other expenses related to attending college/ university?

» Did you receive an financial aid or scholarships? If so, which ones and how did you apply for them?

» Did you work while attending college/university? If so, what kind of job did you have and how many hours did you work per week?

» How did you manage other expenses related to attending college/university, such as textbooks, housing, transportation, and food?

» Did you have to take out any loans to pay for college/university? If so, how much did you borrow and how are you managing your student loan debt now?

» What advice would you give to someone who is currently trying to manage the costs of attending college/university?

TASK 2: CREATE YOUR OWN PODCAST!

You can give your research a creative twist by starting a podcast! Besides gathering relevant information for yourself, you'll be putting it together for others who might need it. We've discussed how valuable and powerful it is to give back to your community, right? This can be how you do it!

Create a podcast where you interview people who have graduated from college/university and ask them about their experiences managing the costs. You can title the podcast "Survival Stories" and ask your guests to share their best tips for staying afloat financially while in school. You can record the interviews and edit them together into a series of episodes, which can be published on a platform like Spotify or Apple Podcasts.

CHAPTER 8

Key takeaways

» Saving for college requires a different level of planning and preparation. There is no doubt that college is a major investment

» College costs: understanding what you're getting into can help you plan ahead and start saving up some cash. It includes not only tuition and fees, but also other expenses like books, supplies, transportation, and even housing.

» Tuition and fees can vary widely depending on the college and the program you choose. Housing is another major expense to consider.

» Prices differ from the different types of colleagues

» Financial aid is money that is given or lent to students in order to help pay for their education. Federal financial aid is money that is given to students by the government in order to help pay for their college tuition and fees.

» Scholarships are a type of financial aid that are awarded to students based on their academic or other achievements, such as athletic ability, community service, or artistic talent.

» A 529 plan gives you tax benefits when you use it to pay for qualified education expenses. Coverdell Education Savings Accounts (ESAs) are tax-advantaged investment accounts designed to help families save for qualified education expenses. Roth IRA and mutual fund, are accounts that may offer more flexibility in terms of how you can use your savings.

» It's important to keep track of your progress of saving by annotating everything, including your expenses, savings, and any contributions you make to your college savings accounts.

» Paying for college requires careful planning and budgeting. Loans and private loans appear here.

» Work-study programs are a form of assistance that allows students to work part-time jobs on campus or off-campus to earn money to help pay for college expenses.

» It's important to remember that choosing a career path is a process, not a one-time decision. You have to consider is your personal interests, values and job outlook

Chapter 9

Retirement Plan

"Retirement is not a time to sit back and watch the world go by. It's time to take action and make a difference."
S. Jay Olshansky

 **LET'S TALK ABOUT RETIREMENT. I KNOW, IT MAY SEEM LIKE A LIFETIME AWAY, BUT TRUST ME, IT'S ALWAYS EARLY ENOUGH TO START PLANNING FOR IT.**

You see, retirement is not something to dread or fear but rather a new chapter in your life that can be just as fulfilling and enjoyable as any other.

You might think, " I'm young, and I don't even have a serious job yet!" That may be true, but your future job and how you handle your money now will directly impact your retirement years. So, it's essential to start learning about retirement planning now.

Think about it, do you really want to spend your golden years bored and stuck at home? I didn't think so. That's why preparing for retirement with time is key. It requires commitment, but it will all be worth it.

Let me give you an example. Have you seen the movie "The Intern" with Robert De Niro? (If you haven't, you should!) He plays a senior intern at a fashion website who takes his job seriously and works hard despite being retired. The movie shows that retirement is not the end of a person's life but rather a new chapter that can be fulfilling and enjoyable.

So, what can you do now to prepare for retirement? First, start thinking about your career and how you can save and invest your money wisely. Educate yourself on retirement plans and start putting money into a retirement account as soon as possible.

I know it may seem overwhelming, but trust me, you'll thank yourself in the future. With some planning and preparation, you can ensure that your retirement years are as exciting and fulfilling as your younger years.

RETIREMENT 101

Retirement may sound like a distant and abstract concept, especially if you are young and just starting your career. But please bear with me; it's better than you think. It is never too early to start planning for yours.

The question is, what does retirement really mean? It is basically the time in someone's life when they decide to stop working because they've reached a certain age and begin relying on accumulated savings, investments, and pensions to support their lifestyle.

Now, the age people retire can vary from country to country. For example, in some places you can retire at 60, while in others, you might have to wait until you're 70. It depends on where you live and what the rules are there.

Regardless of the retirement age where you live, the basic idea is always the same: at some point, you stop working. And that can be exciting for some people, while others might not know what to do with themselves all day.

IMPORTANCE OF RETIREMENT PLANNING

In retirement planning, you prepare for your financial and lifestyle needs. You need to set goals and create a plan to help you achieve them.

You've probably heard countless times that the earlier you start saving for retirement, the better. Having a 40- to 50-year head start on retirement can pay off for you.

It's important to start saving for retirement as early as possible because the earlier you start, the more time you have to grow your savings and the more you can benefit from compounding interest. But this is not enough to convince you; here are some better reasons:

1. Financial Security: Retirement planning helps you save and invest your money wisely to have a secure financial future. By planning ahead and creating a retirement fund, you can ensure you have enough money to cover your expenses during retirement.

2. Peace of Mind: You don't have to worry about running out of money or being unable to afford the lifestyle you want. Instead, you can relax and enjoy your golden years without financial stress.

3. Long-Term Care: Retirement planning also includes considering the cost of long-term care. As you age, you may require medical assistance, and retirement planning ensures you have the resources to cover these expenses.

Overall, retirement planning is crucial for a secure and comfortable retirement. Start planning today to ensure a bright future ahead.

The effects of not planning for retirement

Not planning for retirement means not only making your golden years steeper, but also not taking advantage of the thousands of ways you can enjoy your leave years.

One of the biggest effects of not planning for retirement is financial stress. You'll need money to support yourself when you're older and no longer working. If you have yet to save enough money for retirement, you could struggle to make ends meet. That means you might not be able to do things you want, like travel or take up a new hobby, because you simply need more money for it.

And trust me, you do not want to deal with financial stress when you're older. Retirement is supposed to be a time when you can relax and enjoy your life, not worry about how you will pay the bills.

Another effect of not planning for retirement is that you'll have to cut back on your expenses. This means you might only be able to do some of the things you want to do in your older years. For example, you might need help to travel to new places or take up expensive hobbies.

But it's not just about the money - not planning for retirement can also impact your mental health. If you're constantly worried about money or need help to do the things you want to do, it can be really tough.

PLANNING FOR RETIREMENT IN YOUR TEEN YEARS

But what can you do as a teenager? There is an easy answer to this question: Savings accounts. At this point, you probably are a master of finances and know you can use this type of account for planning, saving, and investing.

STARTING EARLY TO TAKE ADVANTAGE OF COMPOUND INTEREST

To take advantage of the power of compound interest, you need to start saving for your retirement as early as possible. Compound interest is the interest earned not only on the principal amount invested but also on the accumulated interest over time. So, if you start saving early, your money has more time to grow through compound interest.

Over time, the interest earned on your initial investment and accumulated interest can add up significantly. For example, let's say you invest $10,000 at an annual interest rate of 6%. After one year, you will have earned $600 in interest. With simple interest, you would make $600 each year after that. However, with compound interest, the $600 interest you earned in the first year is added to your principal, bringing the total to $10,600. In the second year, you make interest on the new total of $636 ($10,600 x 0.06).

Investing in retirement early allows you to take advantage of compound interest over a longer period of time. For example, if you start saving for retirement at age 25 and contribute $5,000 per year with an average annual return of 6%, you could potentially have over $600,000 saved by age 65. If you wait until age 35 to start saving and contribute the same amount, you would have only about $300,000 saved by age 65.

Even small contributions can add up significantly over time. So, start saving as early as possible to take advantage of the power of compound interest and achieve your retirement goals.

IDENTIFYING RETIREMENT GOALS

Now that you know it's important to start planning for retirement early, let's talk about identifying your retirement goals.

Figuring out what you want to achieve in your older years is a significant first step in retirement planning.

What are some goals you might have for your retirement? Well, the possibilities are endless! Maybe you dream of traveling the world, visiting exotic locations, and experiencing different cultures. Or perhaps you want to buy a second home somewhere peaceful and relaxing, where you can spend your days reading, gardening, or just enjoying the scenery.

Of course, retirement goals don't have to be grandiose or expensive. You may want to spend more time with family and friends or pursue a hobby you're passionate about. Whatever your goals, it is crucial to identify them early on so you can start planning accordingly.

There are several ways you can go about identifying your retirement goals. One approach is to simply sit down and list what you want to do when you're older. This might involve brainstorming with friends or family members or researching to find out what activities and experiences are available to retirees.

Another approach is to think about your values and priorities. What's most important to you in life? Do you value adventure, financial security, or close relationships with loved ones? Your retirement goals should reflect your personal values and priorities.

Once you've identified your retirement goals, you can start thinking about how to achieve them. This might involve saving money, investing in the stock market, or improving your overall financial health.

Whatever approach you take, remember that the key is to start planning early and stay committed to your goals over the long term.

DEVELOPING A LONG-TERM PLAN

Developing a long-term retirement plan is important in ensuring you have comfortable and enjoyable golden years. Here are some tips on creating a long-term strategy that works for you.

The first step is to estimate your retirement expenses. This means figuring out how much money you'll need to cover your basic living expenses and any additional costs associated with your retirement goals. Some common retirement expenses include housing, healthcare, food, transportation, and entertainment. It's important to be as realistic as possible when estimating your expenses to get an accurate picture of how much money you'll need in retirement.

Once you have a good idea of your retirement expenses, it's time to create a savings plan. This plan should outline how much money you need to save each year to reach your retirement goals. Consider investing in tax-advantaged retirement accounts like 401(k) plans, IRAs, and Roth IRAs. These can provide significant tax benefits and help your money grow faster over time.

It's a good idea to review and adjust your plan regularly, perhaps annually. This will help you stay on track and ensure you're doing everything possible to achieve your retirement goals.

Remember, developing a long-term retirement plan is an important investment in your future. It may seem daunting at first, but with careful planning and dedication, you can set yourself up for a comfortable and fulfilling retirement. Good luck!

TYPES OF
RETIREMENT PLANS

There are many ways to plan your retirement. Let's figure out which one is right for you.

SOCIAL SECURITY

Social Security is a federal program that provides retirement, disability, and survivor benefits to eligible individuals. It is funded through payroll taxes and provides a basic retirement income level to supplement other retirement savings sources.

PENSION PLANS

Pension plans are retirement savings sponsored by employers that provide a specific benefit amount to employees upon retirement. They can be defined benefit plans, which provide a specific benefit amount based on factors such as salary and years of service, or defined contribution plans, which allow employees and employers to contribute to a retirement account.

401(K)S

401(k)s are employer-sponsored retirement plans that allow employees to contribute pre-tax dollars to a retirement account. Employers may also offer matching contributions up to a certain amount. The 401(k) funds grow tax-free until they are withdrawn in retirement.

INDIVIDUAL RETIREMENT ACCOUNTS (IRAS)

Individual Retirement Accounts (IRAs) are personal retirement savings accounts that individuals can open and contribute to independently. Traditional IRAs allow individuals to contribute pre-tax dollars and defer taxes until withdrawal in retirement. Roth IRAs, on the other hand, allow individuals to contribute after-tax dollars and withdraw funds tax-free in retirement.

ROTH IRAS

Individual Retirement Accounts (IRAs) are personal retirement savings accounts that individuals can open and contribute to on their own. Traditional IRAs allow individuals to contribute pre-tax dollars and defer taxes until withdrawal in retirement. Roth IRAs, on the other hand, allow individuals to contribute after-tax dollars and withdraw funds tax-free in retirement.

Roth IRAs are similar to traditional IRAs but with some key differences. Roth IRA contributions are made with after-tax dollars, so they do not provide a tax deduction in the year they are made. However, withdrawals from a Roth IRA in retirement are tax-free, including any earnings on the contributions.

Overall, these retirement savings vehicles offer different benefits and considerations, and it's important to consider which options make the most sense for your individual financial situation and retirement goals. A financial advisor can help you navigate these options and make informed decisions.

INVESTMENT OPTIONS
FOR RETIREMENT PLANNING

When it comes to retirement, you can also rely on your investments. This means making the most out of the assets you've made over the years. There are various investment options available for retirement planning.

It's essential to consider your risk tolerance, time horizon, and retirement goals when choosing investments for your retirement plan. Diversification across asset classes can help mitigate risk and provide a balanced portfolio. Working with a financial advisor can help you determine the best investment options for your situation. Here are five standard options:

STOCKS AND MUTUAL FUNDS

Stocks and mutual funds: Stocks and mutual funds can provide long-term growth potential for retirement savings. Stocks are investments in individual companies, while mutual funds are collections of stocks, bonds, or other assets. Both stocks and mutual funds involve risk, as the value of the investments can fluctuate in response to market conditions.

BONDS

Bonds: Bonds are fixed-income investments that can provide a steady income stream in retirement. They can be issued by corporations, municipalities, or the federal government and typically have a fixed interest rate and maturity date.

REAL ESTATE

Real estate investments can offer potential growth and income, particularly through rental properties. However, they also involve risks such as vacancy and maintenance costs and can require significant capital to get started.

ANNUITIES

Annuities are insurance contracts that provide guaranteed payments in exchange for a lump-sum investment or ongoing contributions. They can provide a steady income stream in retirement but may come with fees and restrictions.

SAVINGS ACCOUNTS

Savings accounts and other cash equivalents can provide a safe place to store retirement savings but typically offer lower returns than other investments. They can be useful for short-term savings or as an emergency fund.

To sum it up, retirement planning is an essential aspect of your financial life that should not be overlooked, even as a teenager. Starting early and setting clear goals can help you create a long-term plan that works for you, and can help ensure that you have the financial means to live a comfortable and fulfilling life in retirement. By estimating your expenses, creating a savings plan, and reviewing and adjusting your plan regularly, you can stay on track and make the most of your retirement years. So don't wait any longer, start planning for your retirement today and make the most of your future!

LET'S WORK TOGETHER

WORKSHEET: GOALS FOR RETIREMENT YEARS

In the box below. Describe what you'd like to do when you retire.

With the conclusion of your reflection, set 3 goals.

Describe what you learned in this chapter about retirement in the box below.

Make a Plan of how are you continuing to save for retirement.

Remember: It is important to readjust the plan as you grow.

CHAPTER 9

Key takeaways

» Retirement is basically the time in someone's life when they decide to stop working because they've reached a certain age. The specific age at that people retire can vary from country to country.

» In retirement planning, you prepare for your financial and lifestyle needs. You need to set goals and create a plan to help you achieve them. You get from it financial security, peace of mind, and long-term care

» One of the most significant effects of not planning for retirement is financial stress. You'll have to cut back on your expenses.

» You have to take advantage of the power of compound interest. Compound interest is the interest earned not only on the principal amount invested but also on the accumulated interest over time

» Now that you know it's essential to start planning for retirement early, let's talk about how to identify your retirement goals.

» Developing a long-term retirement plan might seem overwhelming. Still, it's actually an essential step in ensuring that you have a comfortable and enjoyable retirement.

» When planning for retirement, it's essential to consider the impact of inflation and market fluctuations on your savings over time.

Chapter 10

Putting it all together

"If you want to change the world,
change yourself."
Mahatma Gandhi

KNOW THAT FEELING YOU GET WHEN YOU'RE ALMOST AT YOUR DESTINATION ON A ROAD TRIP? THAT MIX OF EXCITEMENT AND SADNESS BECAUSE THE ADVENTURE IS ALMOST OVER, AND YOU'RE UNSURE WHAT TO FEEL? I GET THAT SAME FEELING WHEN GETTING TO THE END OF AN EXCELLENT BOOK.

It's like my stomach is doing backflips because I'm dying to know what gets to the end, but I'm also sad that my journey is almost over. When I finally complete the book, I love looking back at the road I just traveled, feeling both accomplished and a little wistful.

Our journey together is also drawing to a close. Quite a trip it was as well! We're almost at the point of looking back and being shocked by how far we've come, but let's make one last stop before doing so.

As a teenager, you may think you have plenty of time to figure everything out. After all, you're still young and have your whole life ahead of you, right? Well, while it's true that you do have time, it's never too early to start learning about finance and money management. Luckily, you did that already! At this point in the book, you must master the different areas of personal finances. In this last chapter, I want to share my most important secret: The power of setting SMART goals when building financial habits.

If you doubt how powerful SMART goals can be, look at the music queen: Beyoncé. She's a great real-life example of setting smart financial goals. She started her music career as a teenager and quickly became one of the most successful artists ever. She set smart financial goals throughout her career and made wise investments to build her wealth. At different stages of building her wealth, she made the right decisions to get where she wanted to go. She diversified her income streams, investing in ventures such as real estate, clothing lines, and even a vegan meal delivery service.

Beyoncé's fortune wasn't built in a day. It took years of hard work, dedication, and smart financial decisions to get where she is today. Beyoncé's story reminds you that it's never too early to start setting goals and making wise investments.

It's not enough to know. You need to use it to change your reality. In this chapter, we will review some financial terms and set goals for your financial journey. So, grab a pen and paper, get comfortable, and let's dive in!

WHY IT IS ESSENTIAL TO MANAGE YOUR PERSONAL FINANCES IN A SMART WAY

Now that we've covered all the details of finances let's talk about why it's so important to manage your money wisely. Hold up, what does that even mean? It's all about setting smart goals, planning to get there, and building healthy habits. Trust me, when it comes to your hard-earned cash, you wanna be smart about it.

1. For starters, making intelligent decisions about your money helps you take control of your money and make better decisions about how to use it. Good money management habits will help you live within your means, save for the future, and invest wisely. You'll also be able to avoid falling into debt, which can seriously affect your credit score and overall financial health.

2. Moreover, it can help you achieve your financial goals. Whether you want to save up for a new car, go on a dream vacation, or even start your own business, having a solid financial plan can help you reach your goals faster and more efficiently. With every passing day, you can get closer to your goals by budgeting and investing wisely.

3. Lastly, managing your finances is essential because it allows you to handle your financial obligations and responsibilities. Whether it's paying bills, saving for the future, or investing in your education, having control over your finances can help you meet your financial goals and ensure you're prepared for unexpected expenses.

Managing finances is essential for maintaining financial stability, achieving goals, and building a secure future.

FINANCIAL GOALS 101

With everything learned in previous chapters, you can surely move forward in your financial journey. Learning to set smart goals is the next step. Your goals can be short-term, such as saving for a new phone or going on a trip with your friends, or long-term, such as buying a house or saving for retirement. Setting financial goals is crucial because it gives you something to work towards and helps you stay motivated and focused on your financial journey.

SETTING FINANCIAL GOALS

Setting financial goals for yourself is a great way to ensure you're making the most of your money and working towards a brighter financial future. You do it to achieve the things you want.

First, you must start by thinking about what you want to achieve with your money. You may want to save up for a big purchase, like a car or an overseas trip. Or perhaps you're thinking about the future and want to start saving for college or a down payment on a house. Whatever your goals, it's crucial to consider them carefully and ensure they're achievable.

Achievable Goals

- Saving $500 for a new laptop within six months
- Setting aside $100 per month for college tuition
- Creating an emergency fund of $1,000 within a year
- Paying off a credit card debt of $500 in three months
- Saving $1,000 for a study abroad program in two years

Non-Achievable Goals

- Buying a luxury car with a part-time job income
- Owning a mansion by the age of 25
- Investing in the stock market without any prior knowledge or research
- Going on an expensive shopping spree every month
- Buying designer clothes with a minimum wage salary

Remember, setting financial goals is all about being intentional with your money. Good intentions won't get you far. You have to learn SMART goals if you want to see your profits skyrocket. Is there anyone who wouldn't like that?

SMART GOALS

Now that you have understood the importance of setting goals let's focus on how to do it in a SMART way.

SMART is an acronym for Specific, Measurable, Achievable, Relevant, and Time-bound. When setting financial goals, it's crucial to ensure they meet all of these criteria to increase the likelihood of success. Let's break down each of these components:

 Specific: A specific goal is clearly defined and easy to understand. Instead of setting a goal to "save money," you might set a goal to "save $500 for a new laptop."

 Measurable: A measurable goal is one that you can track and quantify. For example, if you aim to save $500 for a new laptop, you can track your progress by checking your savings account balance.

 Achievable: An achievable goal is realistic and attainable based on your current financial situation. For example, if you're currently earning minimum wage, setting a goal to save $10,000 a year is impossible.

 Relevant: A relevant goal aligns with your overall financial plan and priorities. For example, if your goal is to pay off your student loans, setting a goal to save for a new car might be irrelevant.

 Time-bound: A time-bound goal has a specific deadline for completion. This helps to create a sense of urgency and accountability. For example, instead of setting a goal to "save $500 for a new laptop," you might set a goal to "save $500 for a new laptop by the end of the year."

Setting SMART financial goals can create a clear roadmap for achieving your financial objectives. Remember, achieving your financial goals takes time and effort, but by breaking them down into manageable steps, you can increase your chances of success. At the end of the chapter, you'll find some tools to take time to reflect on your financial situation and set some SMART goals to help you move toward a more financially secure future.

I HAVE MY SMART GOALS; NOW WHAT?

It's time to create a plan to achieve them!

It's essential to start by prioritizing your goals based on their importance and urgency. For example, suppose you have a credit card debt that is accruing interest. In that case, prioritizing paying off that debt might be a good idea before saving for a new car.

Once you've prioritized your goals, it's time to create a plan. This plan should include specific steps and timelines for achieving each goal.

Creating a plan to achieve your goals is a crucial step in becoming financially responsible. This is basically about breaking into achievable steps the process of getting where you want to go.

Here are some tips for creating a plan to achieve your financial goals:

» Break down each goal into smaller, more manageable steps. This will make it easier to track your progress and stay motivated.

» Set specific deadlines for each step of the plan. This will help you stay accountable and ensure that you're making progress toward your goals.

» Stay flexible and adjust your plan as needed. Life is unpredictable, and unexpected expenses or changes in circumstances can derail even the best-laid plans.

YOUR FINANCIAL GOAL IS TO SAVE $2,000 FOR A SUMMER TRIP TO EUROPE.

Here's an example of how you could break down that goal into smaller, more manageable steps:

» Determine how much you need to save each month. If you have six months to save, you'll need to set aside about $333 each month.

» Look for ways to cut back on expenses to free up money for savings. For example, you could bring lunch to school instead of eating out or cancel a subscription service you don't use.

» Open a separate savings account specifically for your Europe trip savings. This will help you keep track of your progress and resist the temptation to dip into those funds for other expenses.

» Set specific deadlines for each monthly savings goal. For example, you could plan to save $100 by the end of the first month, $500 by the end of the third month, and so on.

» Stay flexible and adjust your plan if unexpected expenses or changes in circumstances arise. You can increase your monthly savings goal if you get a part-time job that pays more than you expected. On the other hand, if your car needs unexpected repairs, you may need to adjust your savings plan temporarily.

By breaking down your financial goal into smaller steps, setting specific deadlines, and staying flexible, you can create a plan that's achievable and keeps you motivated along the way.

As you can see, the little things add up and can help you achieve your financial goals. So keep the focus on your financial habits because they're the secret sauce to your success!

GOOD FINANCIAL HABITS

Good financial habits are about more than just making money; they're also about developing a healthy relationship with money. Luckily, you'll be naturally building healthy financial habits when you put into practice the concepts we've covered in the book.

It's essential to understand that money is a tool that can help you achieve your goals and live the life you want, but it's not the only thing that matters. Good financial habits involve finding a balance between spending and saving and understanding that it's okay to treat yourself once in a while.

Having good financial habits also means being intentional about your spending and making conscious decisions about how you use your money. This might involve creating a budget, tracking your expenses, and avoiding unnecessary expenses whenever possible.

TIPS FOR DEVELOPING AND MAINTAINING GOOD FINANCIAL HABITS

Developing and maintaining good financial habits can be challenging, but with the right approach, it's definitely achievable. Here are some tips to help you get started:

1. Assess your current financial habits: The first step to developing good financial habits is to take a hard look at your current habits and identify areas where you can improve. You may be spending too much on unnecessary expenses or not saving enough. Whatever it is, be honest about where you can improve.

2. Set achievable goals to improve your habits: Once you've identified areas to improve, set achievable goals for yourself. Remember to use the SMART goal-setting framework to ensure your goals are specific, measurable, achievable, relevant, and time-bound.

3. Practice discipline and consistency: Good financial habits require discipline and consistency. This means sticking to your budget, avoiding unnecessary expenses, and making conscious decisions about your spending and saving. In this point, you should consider the " Only once" rule.

"Only once" rule

Here's a little rule to live by the "Only Once" rule. It means it's okay to slip up and forget something once in a while - we're only human, after all! But the key is to not let that mistake become a habit. So, don't stress too much if you accidentally blow your budget one day. Just ensure it doesn't happen again the next day or the day after. By sticking to the "Only Once" rule, you can avoid bad habits and stay on track toward your financial goals.

Developing good financial habits takes time and effort, but the rewards are worth it. Start today, and watch as your financial future grows brighter!

LET'S WORK TOGETHER 🖊

Activity 1:

Fill in the blank spaces and make your own SMART goal!

Smart Goals!

SPECIFIC

¿What do you want to accomplish?

MEASURABLE

¿How do you plan to track your goal?

ACHIEVABLE

¿Is it realistic? ¿How do plan to achieve it?

RELEVANT

On the scale from 1 to 10 how relevant is for you this goal

TIME-BOUND

¿How long it will take to achieve his goal?

FINAL GOAL

Activity 2:

Circle the goals that are SMART (and explain why).

→ I will save $5,000 for a down payment on a house by the end of the year by setting aside $417 every month from my paycheck.

→ I want to learn a new language.

→ I want to be rich someday.

→ Earn Ten Thousand Dollars this year.

→ I will run a 10K race in under 50 minutes in six months by following a training plan, eating a healthy diet, and getting enough rest.

→ I want to lose weight

→ I will earn a promotion to manager within the next 12 months by completing additional training courses, taking on more responsibilities, and receiving positive feedback from my supervisor.

→ Stop using the phone so much.

→ Run a marathon at the end of the year.

CHAPTER 10

Key takeaways

» Personal finance management is important because it helps you understand your financial situation, make informed decisions, and plan for the future. By managing your money well, you can avoid unnecessary stress and anxiety and enjoy financial freedom.

» You gain motivation and direction when you set achievable financial goals. When setting goals, it is important to make sure they are realistic and specific, and to create a plan to achieve them.

» SMART goals are specific, measurable, achievable, relevant, and time-bound.

» You can focus your efforts and resources on the things that matter most by prioritizing your financial goals. By creating a list and ranking your goals in order of importance, you can develop a clear plan for achieving them.

» Developing good financial habits helps you build a positive relationship with money and make smart financial decisions. This includes things like budgeting, saving, and investing wisely. Maintaining them is key because it helps you stay on track and achieve your financial goals. This requires discipline and consistency, but it can lead to long-term financial success.

» Money is a useful resource, but it is important to remember that it is not everything. Happiness and fulfillment come from a variety of sources, including relationships, hobbies, and personal growth.

» A valuable way to gain insight and inspiration is to learn from others who have successfully managed their money. Examples include successful entrepreneurs, financial experts, and friends or family members who have made smart financial decisions.

Conclusion

"Tell me, and I forget, teach me and I may
remember, involve me, and I learn."
Benjamin Franklin

CONGRATULATIONS, YOU'VE REACHED THE END OF OUR JOURNEY! IT'S BEEN A FUN RIDE, HASN'T IT? LET ME SHARE A FEW WORDS OF WISDOM BEFORE YOU GO YOUR WAY.

Taking control of your finances early is essential. You should be proud of yourself for taking the time to learn about managing your money. It's not always the most exciting topic, but it's one of the most significant things you can do to secure your future. Believe it or not, this is only the beginning. You now have the tools and knowledge to take control of your finances and build a bright financial future.

Remember those basic concepts from the first chapter that may have seemed a bit dull? Well, they were the foundation for your financial literacy. From there, we explored budgeting, saving and investing, debt management, and giving back to your community. You've come a long way and should be proud of your progress.

But there's still more to learn and do. Building good financial habits and a positive mindset is essential for long-term success. We've discussed goal-setting, budgeting, and financial planning for college and retirement. And with all the investment strategies we've covered, you will find one that works for you. All you have to do is get started!

So what's next? It's up to you to take action and implement what you've learned. Start small, set achievable goals, and build momentum. This may all seem overwhelming at first but don't worry. Rome wasn't built in a day, and neither is financial success. Remember, every small decision counts. With dedication and perseverance, you can turn your financial dreams into reality.

Last but not least, don't be afraid to ask for help. There are plenty of resources available to help you navigate the world of finance, whether it's a trusted family member, a financial advisor, or even coming back to this book. So don't be shy; ask questions and seek advice when you need it.

Remember, managing your money effectively isn't just for adults. It's something everyone should learn, no matter their age. Don't wait until it's too late. Start implementing what you've learned today and watch your money grow. The saying goes, "The best time to plant a tree was 20 years ago. The second-best time is now." Don't wait any longer to start your journey toward financial success!

Remember to reach out to
aemerdale@gmail.com
for your free answer sheet!

GLOSSARY

401(k): A retirement savings plan offered by many employers in the United States. It allows employees to contribute a portion of their salary to a tax-advantaged investment account.

Assets: Items of value that you own, such as cash, property, investments, or possessions like a car or jewelry.

ATM: Short for Automated Teller Machine, it is a self-service machine that allows you to perform banking transactions, such as withdrawing cash, making deposits, or checking your account balance.

Bankruptcy: A legal status of being unable to repay debts owed to creditors. Bankruptcy provides a fresh start but has long-term consequences on creditworthiness.

Bear Market: A market condition where prices of securities, such as stocks, are falling or expected to fall. It is often characterized by widespread pessimism and selling pressure.

Budget: A plan that helps you manage your money by tracking your income and expenses. It allows you to allocate funds for different needs and helps you save and spend wisely.

Bull Market: A market condition where prices of securities, such as stocks, are rising or expected to rise. It is often characterized by optimism and buying pressure.

Capital Expenditure: Money spent by a company to acquire, upgrade, or maintain long-term assets, such as property, equipment, or technology, that will benefit the business over an extended period.

Capital Gain: The profit earned from selling a capital asset, such as stocks, bonds, or real estate, at a price higher than the purchase price. It is subject to capital gains tax.

Capital: Financial assets or resources used to generate income or invest in ventures. It can refer to money, property, or other valuable assets.

Capitalism: An economic system characterized by private ownership of resources and means of production, where individuals and businesses operate for profit and compete in the marketplace.

Cash Flow: The movement of money in and out of your accounts, tracking how much money you receive and spend over a specific period. Positive cash flow means you have more money coming in than going out.

Certificate of Deposit (CD): A time deposit offered by banks and credit unions that pays a fixed interest rate over a specific period. CDs typically have a higher interest rate than regular savings accounts but require the funds to be locked in for a predetermined term.

Collateral: An asset or property pledged as security for a loan. If the borrower fails to repay the loan, the lender can seize and sell the collateral to recover their money.

Compound Annual Growth Rate (CAGR): The average annual rate of return over a specific period, considering the compounding effect. It provides a standardized measure of investment performance.

Compound Interest: Interest that is calculated not only on the initial amount but also on any interest previously earned. It allows your savings or investments to grow at an accelerated rate over time.

Credit Card: A payment card that allows you to borrow money from a bank or financial institution up to a certain credit limit. You can make purchases and repay the borrowed amount later, either in full or through monthly installments.

Credit Report: A detailed record of an individual's credit history, including information about loans, credit cards, and payment history. Credit reports are used by lenders to assess creditworthiness.

Credit Score: A numerical representation of your creditworthiness based on your credit history. Lenders use this score to determine your creditworthiness when you apply for loans or credit.

Credit: A borrowing arrangement that allows you to use someone else's money temporarily, with the promise to repay it later. It often involves the use of credit cards or loans.

Debit Card: A payment card linked to your bank account that allows you to make purchases or withdraw cash. The funds are deducted directly from your account.

Debt: Money owed to someone else, often obtained through loans or credit. It's important to manage debt responsibly to avoid financial difficulties.

Depreciation: The decrease in the value of an asset over time due to factors such as wear and tear, age, or obsolescence. It is often accounted for in financial statements and can affect the resale value of an asset.

Diversification: Spreading your investments across different asset classes (stocks, bonds, real estate, etc.) to reduce risk. It helps to minimize the impact of any single investment performing poorly.

Dividends: A portion of a company's profits distributed to shareholders as a return on their investment. Dividends are typically paid out regularly, often on a quarterly basis.

Emergency Fund: A savings account set aside for unexpected expenses or emergencies, such as medical bills or car repairs. It provides a financial safety net and helps avoid taking on debt in times of crisis.

Entrepreneur: A person who starts and runs their own business, often taking on financial risks in pursuit of a profitable venture.

Entrepreneurship: The act of starting and managing one's own business, taking on financial risks in hopes of generating profits and creating innovative solutions.

Equity: The ownership interest or value that an individual or entity has in an asset, such as a house or business, after deducting any outstanding liabilities.

Expenses: The money you spend on various things, including necessities like food, clothing, and transportation, as well as discretionary items like entertainment and hobbies.

FICO Score: A credit score calculated by the Fair Isaac Corporation (FICO) that is widely used by lenders to evaluate your creditworthiness. It is based on factors such as your payment history, amounts owed, length of credit history, and more.

Financial Goal: A specific objective you set for your financial future. Examples include saving for college, buying a car, or building a retirement fund.

Financial Literacy: The knowledge and understanding of financial concepts and skills necessary to make informed financial decisions. It involves managing money, budgeting, saving, investing, and understanding financial products and services.

Freelance Gig: A short-term, project-based work arrangement where individuals work independently for various clients without long-term employment contracts. Examples include graphic design, writing, or web development.

Freelancing: Providing services or completing projects for multiple clients on a self-employed basis. Freelancers are typically responsible for managing their own taxes, invoicing, and business expenses.

Frugal: Being mindful of spending and avoiding unnecessary expenses. Frugality is about making wise financial choices and maximizing the value of each dollar.

Grants: Financial aid or funds provided by government agencies, institutions, or organizations to support individuals or businesses for specific purposes, such as education, research, or community development.

Gross Domestic Product (GDP): The total value of all goods and services produced within a country's borders in a specific period. GDP is used as an indicator of a country's economic health.

Gross Income: The total amount of income earned before any deductions, such as taxes or retirement contributions, are subtracted.

Identity Theft: The fraudulent use of someone's personal information without their consent, often for financial gain. It's important to protect your personal information and be cautious of online scams and phishing attempts.

Income: The money you receive on a regular basis, such as wages from a job, allowance, or any other source of financial inflow.

Inflation Rate: The percentage increase in the average price level of goods and services over time. It erodes the purchasing power of money and affects the cost of living.

Inflation: The gradual increase in the prices of goods and services over time. Inflation reduces the purchasing power of money, meaning the same amount of money buys less in the future.

Inheritance: Money or assets received from a deceased person's estate. It is often passed on to beneficiaries named in a will or determined by laws of inheritance.

Initial Public Offering (IPO): The first sale of a company's stock to the public. It allows the company to raise capital by offering ownership shares to investors.

Insurance: A contract that provides financial protection against certain risks or losses. It involves paying a premium to an insurance company in exchange for coverage.

Interest Rate: The percentage charged for borrowing money or the amount earned on deposited funds over a specific period. It affects the cost of borrowing or the return on savings.

Interest: The fee charged for borrowing money or the amount earned on deposited funds. It's a percentage of the borrowed or deposited amount and is typically expressed as an annual rate.

Investment: Allocating money into assets like stocks, bonds, or real estate with the expectation of generating income or appreciation over time.

Liabilities: Financial obligations or debts that you owe to others, such as loans, credit card balances, or mortgages.

Liquidity: The ease with which an asset or investment can be converted into cash without significant loss of value. Cash is considered the most liquid asset.

Minimum Wage: The legally mandated lowest hourly wage that employers must pay workers. Minimum wage laws vary by jurisdiction.

Mortgage Refinancing: The process of obtaining a new mortgage with more favorable terms to replace an existing mortgage. Refinancing can help lower monthly payments, reduce interest rates, or change the loan's duration.

Mortgage: A loan provided by a bank or financial institution to help you purchase a home. It is secured by the property you buy and is repaid over a specified period, usually through monthly mortgage payments.

Mutual Fund: A type of investment vehicle that pools money from multiple investors to invest in a diversified portfolio of stocks, bonds, or other securities. It offers individual investors access to a professionally managed and diversified investment.

Net Income: The amount of income remaining after deductions, such as taxes and other expenses, are subtracted from your gross income.

Net Worth: The difference between your total assets and liabilities. It provides a snapshot of your financial health and indicates your overall financial standing.

Overdraft: Occurs when you spend more money than you have available in your bank account. It can result in fees and additional charges, so it's important to manage your account balance carefully.

Payday Loan: A short-term, high-interest loan intended to cover expenses until the borrower's next paycheck. Payday loans often come with high fees and should be used as a last resort due to their high cost.

Payroll Deduction: The automatic deduction of certain expenses or contributions from an employee's paycheck, such as taxes, retirement contributions, or health insurance premiums.

Philanthropy: The act of donating money, resources, or time to charitable causes or organizations that aim to help others or address social issues.

Portfolio: A collection of investments, such as stocks, bonds, mutual funds, and other assets, held by an individual or entity. Diversifying your portfolio can help manage risk.

Prepaid Card: A payment card that is loaded with a specific amount of money in advance. It can be used to make purchases until the loaded balance is depleted.

Real Estate Investment Trust (REIT): A company that owns, operates, or finances income-generating real estate properties. REITs allow investors to invest in real estate without directly owning properties.

Recession: A significant decline in economic activity, characterized by a contraction in the gross domestic product (GDP), increased unemployment, and reduced consumer spending. Recessions are part of the economic cycle.

Recurring Payment: An automatic, regular payment made at fixed intervals for services or subscriptions. Examples include monthly utility bills or streaming service subscriptions.

Retirement Savings: Money set aside for your future when you're no longer working. It is important to start saving for retirement early to take advantage of compound interest and ensure financial security later in life.

Return on Investment (ROI): A measure of the profitability of an investment. It calculates the percentage gain or loss on an investment relative to the amount invested.

Return: The financial gain or loss on an investment, usually expressed as a percentage of the initial investment. A positive return indicates a profit, while a negative return represents a loss.

Risk Management: The process of identifying, assessing, and mitigating risks to minimize potential losses or negative impacts. It involves making informed decisions and implementing strategies to protect against financial risks.

Risk: The potential for loss or uncertainty associated with an investment or financial decision. Generally, higher-risk investments have the potential for higher returns but also higher losses.

Roth IRA: A type of individual retirement account (IRA) that allows you to contribute after-tax income and potentially withdraw earnings tax-free in retirement. It offers tax advantages for long-term savings.

Saving: Setting aside a portion of your income for future use or emergencies. It's important to save money to achieve financial goals and be prepared for unexpected expenses.

Stock Exchange: A marketplace where buyers and sellers trade shares of publicly listed companies. It provides liquidity and establishes fair market prices for stocks.

Stock Market: A market where shares of publicly traded companies are bought and sold. Investing in stocks allows you to become a partial owner of a company and potentially earn returns through dividends or capital appreciation.

Student Loans: Loans specifically designed to help students pay for higher education expenses. They typically have lower interest rates and flexible repayment options.

Tax Deduction: An expense or itemized amount that reduces taxable income, thereby lowering the amount of tax owed. Common deductions include mortgage interest, charitable donations, and certain business expenses.

Taxes: Compulsory financial contributions levied by the government on individuals and businesses to fund public services and infrastructure.

Term Life Insurance: A life insurance policy that provides coverage for a specific term, typically 10, 20, or 30 years. If the insured person dies during the term, the beneficiaries receive a death benefit.

Trade-off: The act of giving up one thing to gain another. In financial decision-making, it involves considering the benefits and drawbacks of different options before making a choice.

REVIEW TIME

DID YOU ENJOY THIS BOOK?

We know you know everything about money; we get it.

But we think it's time that you dive into
the Ultimate Investment Workbook,
designed exclusively for savvy minds. 🚀

🎇 Uncover the secrets to turn your pocket
change into serious gains, all while
rocking that #FinancialFreedom vibe. 💸🏃

Whether you're dreaming of the latest tech,
cool travel spots, or just securing your future
swag, this workbook's got your back.

Turn those virtual coins into stacks you can flex,
and remember, future billionaires aren't born –
they're made by taking smart steps today.

So, grab your favorite caffeinated beverage, park
yourself in your comfiest hangout nook, and let's crack
open this workbook of financial awesomeness.

Made in the USA
Las Vegas, NV
09 January 2024

84043901R00096